FRIENDS OF GANDHI

FRIENDS OF GANDHI

Correspondence of Mahatma Gandhi With Esther Faering (Menon) Anne Marie Peterson and Ellen Horu

Edited by

E.S. REDDY and HOLGER TERP

KALPAZ

ISBN : 978-81-8745-812-8

First Published, 2018

Published by

Kalpaz Publications
C-30, Satyawati Nagar,
Delhi – 110052
Ph.: 011-47034999, 9811692060
www.kalpazpublications.com
E-mail: kalpaz@hotmail.com

Printed at: G. Print Process, Delhi

Contents

1. Miss Esther Faering married E. Kuhni Menon in 1921.
2. Including her letters to associates of Gandhi and Gandhi's letters to her daughters, Nan and Tangai.

3. Mahadev (or Mahadeo) Haribhai Desai, secretary to Gandhi.

4. Miss Faering married Mr. Kuhni Menon in 1921.

5. Devadas (or Devdas) Gandhi, fourth and youngest son of Mahatma Gandhi.

6. Gandhi's secretary.
7. Gandhi's associate who acted as his secretary for some time.

Introduction

While doing research on Gandhi's contacts with people outside India, I was surprised to find that he had corresponded with many men and women from Nordic countries. I had known of his letters to Miss Esther Faering (later Mrs. Menon) as Navajivan published them in 1956 under the title *My Dear Child*–but not of letters to or from others. I could not even find biographical information about Miss Faering except what could be derived from the letters.

I compiled the letters of Gandhi to people in Nordic countries and to people from Nordic countries in India, mostly missionaries, from the *Collected Works of Mahatma Gandhi*, as well as letters to him, which were available in the Gandhi archives in Ahmedabad and the National Gandhi Museum in New Delhi. I was anxious to contact a Nordic scholar to obtain information about the correspondents and was referred to Frede Højgaard, a historian who had edited a publication of the Nordic Institute of Asian Studies (NIAS) on Nordic contacts with Gandhi.[8] I hoped to meet him on a visit to Copenhagen but found that he had passed away at an early age.

Fortunately, some time later, Christian Bartolf of the Gandhi Information Center in Berlin introduced me to Holger Terp who had written an article on "Ellen Hørup and Mohandas Gandhi" for the NIAS publication. A librarian who had retired because of poor eyesight, Mr. Terp was a conscientious objector who had been active in the peace movement. He was a co-founder of the Danish

8. Frede Højgaard (ed.) *Friends of Gandhi: Inter-war Scandinavian Responses to the Mahatma*. NIAS Report No. 7. Copenhagen: Nordic Institute of Asian Studies, 1991.

Peace Academy and has edited its website since 2000. He was a godsend to me.

He did an enormous amount of research about the correspondents of Gandhi and on Nordic interest in Gandhi and India, and traced valuable material in the Danish libraries and archives, including some correspondence of Gandhi that was not available in India.

He put up all the correspondence we collected, together with biographical information on the correspondents and available photographs, on the website of:

The Danish Peace Academy
www.fredsakademiet.dk/library/nordic/

This book contains the correspondence of Gandhi with three Danish women–Esther (Faering) Menon, Anne Marie Petersen and Ellen Hørup—who admired him as a person and supported the movement he led for the independence of India. The intimate friendship of Gandhi with these women is a significant episode in the relations between India and Denmark.

Two of the women–Miss Petersen and Miss Faering (later Mrs. Menon)--were devout Christians who had arrived in India as missionaries. They visited Gandhi's *ashram* at Kocharab, Ahmedabad, for three days in January 1917 to observe the school there, and were greatly impressed by Gandhi and the spirit of the *ashram*. Gandhi too developed a fondness for them. He wrote to Esther soon after they left: "You were hardly guests to us; you had become members of the family". He invited them to visit the *ashram* whenever they could. From this encounter developed a close attachment of the two women to Gandhi, as well as their support to his campaigns for social reform and for freedom of India. They were among the few Europeans who demonstrated solidarity with the non-violent resistance of the Indian people at that early stage, despite the hostility of the Christian missions and the British authorities.

Gandhi had returned to India in January 1915 after twenty-one years in South Africa where he had led the resistance of Indian settlers against discriminatory and humiliating treatment by the white rulers. The non-violent campaign of defiance against unjust laws (*satyagraha*) which he led from 1906 to 1914, and in which many thousands of people in the small community suffered imprisonment and brutality and finally won their demands, was to become the model for the struggle of the people of India for independence and for many other oppressed peoples around the world.

Gandhi spent the first two years after his return to India traveling around the country and getting to know India rather than in political activity. He set up an *ashram* at Kocharab, in Ahmedabad, in May 1915, and named it *Satyagrahashram*. Among the inmates were a number of children, mainly boys, who had been brought to India from his South African *ashram* at Phoenix near Durban. The *ashram* was small with only 25 inmates to start with and the living conditions were poor. It was moved in 1917 to a better site on the banks of the Sabarmati River, which the two Danish women visited.

From 1917 Gandhi began to lead non-violent campaigns in India. In 1917, he organised a national campaign against the export of Indian labour, under indenture, to work in semi-slave conditions in plantations in the Caribbean, Mauritius, South Africa and Fiji; and went to Champaran district in Bihar province to help the peasants to secure an end to ruthless exploitation in the indigo plantations. In 1918 he led a no-tax movement in the Kaira district in Gujarat in protest against the refusal by the government to suspend land revenue when the crops had failed. In the same year he guided a strike by workers in textile mills in Ahmedabad.

While these campaigns drew attention to the efficacy of mass non-violent resistance, a bigger challenge was to come soon.

In 1919, when India was expecting greater self-government, the British authorities introduced stringent repressive legislation (known as Rowlatt bills), ostensibly to deal with the revolutionary movement. Gandhi decided on a *satyagraha* against the Rowlatt bills and addressed protest meetings around the country.

About the same time, the British government promulgated restrictions, more severe than during wartime, on Christian missions and individual missionaries. The missions were required to sign a declaration that they would refrain from political activity and exert their influence in loyal cooperation with the colonial government. Individual missionaries were required to give various undertakings, one of which stressed the obligation of teachers to instill loyalty to the government in the minds of pupils.

The Rowlatt bills became law on March 18, 1919, and Gandhi called for a work stoppage, prayer and fasting on 9 April. While the protests were peaceful all over the country, there was some violence in Delhi and Gandhi proceeded there to restore peace. The government prohibited him from entering Delhi and the Punjab province where massive demonstrations were being held. He was arrested on April 9, 1919, when he announced defiance of the order. (This was the first of his many arrests in India). Although he was released in Bombay after two days, hundreds of thousands of people continued protests.

On April 13, 1919, troops under the command of General Reginald Dyer shot at unarmed people at a mass meeting at Jallianwala Bagh in Amritsar, a city in the Punjab; 379 persons were killed and 1,137 injured. This massacre was followed with the imposition of martial law, public floggings and other brutalities.

When the authorities did not take appropriate measures to make amends for this terror in the Punjab and to end repression all over the country, Gandhi and the Indian National Congress decided to mobilise the nation for resistance. They supported the protests by the Muslim community against Britain's betrayal of promises concerning the treatment of Turkey and the Caliphate at the end of the World War. Gandhi launched a "non-cooperation movement" in 1920, which in its first stage involved boycott of courts and schools, the establishment of national schools and the return of decorations and titles to the government. The next stage was the burning of foreign cloth, as imports of cloth had led to the unemployment of millions of people in India and caused enormous poverty, and promotion of *Khadi* (handspun and hand-woven cloth). This movement was perhaps the most widespread non-violent resistance until that time.

Petersen, he was "the great saint" and "beloved leader". To Mrs. Hørup, he gave "what I have been seeking all my life".

They had differences with Gandhi. Miss Faering, as a devout Christian, could not agree with Gandhi that all religions are equally true, or, to quote him, that "truth is the same in all religions though through refraction it appears for the time being variegated even as light does through a prism".[11] Miss Petersen was anxious that India should be converted to Christianity. She wrote to a friend in 1921:

> "I can only live in the hope that India as a people will become Christian, be born again and be able to play its role in the history of the world as a liberated nation..."[12]

Gandhi did not try to convert them to his faith and the differences did not affect their respect for each other. He wrote to Esther (then Mrs. Menon) on September 17, 1926:

> "In spite of most devout attention to every word ascribed to Jesus in the New Testament and in spite of my having read in a humble spirit all about Jesus, I have really not seen any fundamental distinction between him and the other great teachers. That you see a vast difference between Jesus and the other teachers I can understand, explain and appreciate. That is the teaching you have imbibed from childhood... But this is not a matter for argument. It is a matter for each one's deep and sacred conviction. I have no desire whatsoever to dislodge you from the exclusive homage you pay to Jesus. But I would like you to understand and appreciate the other inclusive position."[13]

Mrs. Hørup too became critical of Gandhi's views on several subjects, but that did not diminish her admiration for Gandhi.

Gandhi was open-minded. He paid attention to the views of the three women, and invited discussion. After answering a question

11. Letter to Miss Esther Faering, December 7, 1919.
12. Letter to Marius Olsen, quoted in Bent Smidt Hansen, *Dependency and Identity*, page 181.
13. Letter to Mrs. Esther (Faering) Menon, September 17, 1926.

by Miss Faering on non-violence, he wrote: "Do please write and fight every inch of the ground that to you may appear untenable. That will enable me to find the way".[14]

Almost all the letters by Gandhi in this book, as well as annotations to them, are from the *Collected Works of Mahatma Gandhi*. We have added additional information obtained from our researches. The dates are as indicated in the *Collected Works*.

Unfortunately, only a fraction of the letters to Gandhi has been preserved. We are grateful to Gandhi Smarak Sangrahalaya at *Harijan Ashram*, Ahmedabad, and to the National Gandhi Museum in New Delhi, for providing copies of letters to Gandhi.[15] A few words or passages in these letters could not be transcribed.

We would invite readers who desire further information on Gandhi and the Nordic countries to refer to the website of:

The Danish Peace Academy
www.fredsakademiet.dk/library/nordic/

I wish to express my great appreciation to Holger Terp for his collaboration and to Christian Bartolf for his constant encouragement in the preparation of this book.

E. S. Reddy
New York

January 2006

14. Letter to Miss Esther Faering, June 30, 1918.
15. The letters from the archive at the *Harijan Ashram* have a number with the suffix SN.

ESTHER FAERING (MENON), 1889-1962

Biographical Note

Miss Esther Faering (born in Copenhagen, June 22, 1889) arrived in India in 1915 as a teacher on the staff of the Danish Missionary Society (DMS) in the Madras Presidency.[16] She shared a flat with Miss Anne Marie Petersen for some time and developed a close friendship with her.

Miss Petersen was entrusted by the DMS with the preparation of plans to establish a high school for girls and was authorised to visit a number of educational institutions in India. She took Miss Faering on the tour. The two women arrived at Gandhi's *ashram* at Kocharab, Ahmedabad, on January 6, 1917, and spent three days there. They developed great admiration for Gandhi, his *ashram* and its ideals. Miss Faering, in particular, developed a strong attachment to Gandhi.

16. After independence of India, Madras Presidency was divided into linguistic states. The Danish Missionary Society had operated in what is now "Tamil Nadu".

After returning to her position as teacher in a girls' boarding school at Tirukoilur, Miss Faering tried to live as an inmate of the *ashram*, wearing *Khadi* and becoming a vegetarian. She wrote frequently to Gandhi, followed his activities and began to identify herself with India and its struggle for freedom. Gandhi treated her as a daughter and wrote often, replying to her letters and keeping her informed of his work. This was a period when Gandhi led a successful *satyagraha* (passive resistance) of peasants against rapacious indigo planters at Champaran in the Bihar province.

Miss Faering came under severe pressure from the DMS and the British authorities because of her attachment to Gandhi. She had to face these pressures alone, as Miss Petersen was away in Denmark from 1917 to 1919 to canvass support for the girls' school.

The Board of the DMS disapproved of her frequent correspondence with Gandhi, and prohibited her from visiting Gandhi's *ashram* during Christmas 1917. She was very disappointed, but Gandhi advised her to be patient and obey the terms of her contract with the Mission.

The missionary authorities became more restrictive in 1918 and tried to persuade her to stop all correspondence with Gandhi. They again prohibited her from going to the *ashram*. At the suggestion of C.F. Andrews,[17] she went to Santiniketan, the school established by Rabindranath Tagore in Bengal, and taught English.

In 1919 Gandhi was engaged in organising national mass resistance against repression by the British authorities. Miss Faering not only refused to dissociate from Gandhi but identified herself even more with Gandhi and India.

She wrote to Mahadev Desai, secretary to Gandhi, on March 24, 1919:

17. Charles Freer Andrews (1871-1940), a British churchman who taught at Santiniketan, was a friend and close associate of Gandhi and poet Rabindranath Tagore.

"When I came to India, I felt at once at home; and here I have found my living ideal, the incarnation of God in man. So next to the great experience when Christ became a living reality in my life, I have no other event for which I am so happy and thankful as the day when I first met *Bapu*; here I found the divine love shining forth clearer than the brightest star; and truth and humanity I found in him as nowhere else, and so I bow down in deepest reverence, love and admiration for true greatness. *Bapu* became for me the manifestation of the love of God and His aim with regard to man, so he came into my life as the living ideal, for which I have been seeking for years".

Gandhi, too, developed a great attachment to Miss Faering and showed great concern for her welfare. Even when he was being taken from Delhi to Bombay[18] under arrest, he wrote a letter to reassure her.

Miss Faering came under suspicion by the authorities and was concerned that she would be deported. She wrote to Mahadev Desai on May 4, 1919:

"The C.I.D.[19] has inquired in Tirukoilur if I had anything to do with the Sg,[20] and if I was the one who brought those school-girls in Villupuram St.[21] For me they can do as they like, only as I said often before, I should rather stay several years in prison than leave India; I do not know how I should live outside India without having my heart completely here".

In June 1919, under pressure from the British authorities, the head of the DMS in India asked her to cease all correspondence with all who were in any way connected with any political work.

18. Now "Mumbai".
19. Central Intelligence Department of the Police.
20. *Satyagraha*?
21. Station.

In the same month, she met E. Kuhni Menon, a Hindu medical student from Kerala, and they were soon engaged to be married. That created general opposition in the Mission and she submitted her resignation on August 6, 1919. The Mission asked her to leave for Denmark but she refused "as I belong to India today more than ever before".

Gandhi wrote to the Governors of Bombay and Madras requesting them to allow her to live in his *ashram* and assured them that he had not the slightest desire to avail himself of her services in the political field.[22] He wrote to the Governor of Bombay:

> "... I believe she is attached to me like a child to its father, simply because, in her opinion, I represent in action the ideals she would fain enforce in her own life and is ever trying to. She loves India as her own motherland and I know it would be a terrible wrench to her if she is ever banished from India, as she dreads she might... I believe her to be as truthful and straight a person as is to be found anywhere. She ever lives in the fear of God and does her best to live a Christian life".[23]

He requested his friend, C.F. Andrews, to go immediately to Madras[24] and do what he could to prevent her banishment. He wrote to Andrews on August 22:

> "I do want you to agree with me that it is just as important to do our best to protect Miss Faering from harm as it is for me to resist the Rowlatt Act with my life and for you to be at Santiniketan".

Miss Faering received permission to travel to the Bombay Presidency and arrived at the *ashram* in October. But Gandhi

22. Ahmedabad, the site of the *ashram*, was then within the Bombay Presidency. After independence the Presidency was divided into linguistic states and Ahmedabad is now in Gujarat state.
23. SN6843; *Collected Works*, Volume 16, pages 57-58.
24. Now "Chennai".

had to leave the *ashram* soon after her arrival on a tour of the Punjab because of the grave political situation in that province. From there he had to go to Delhi to bring about peace. Gandhi and Miss Faering corresponded frequently, but could not meet.

Miss Faering went to Madras to spend Christmas 1919 with Miss Petersen who had returned from Denmark. When she returned to the *ashram* in January, Gandhi had to leave again on a tour.

Miss Faering's health deteriorated and she left for Madras in February 1920 to recuperate. In the same month, she announced her betrothal to Kuhni Menon, possibly in the hope that it would facilitate permission for her to stay in India. His family was opposed to the marriage and there was a storm of criticism from the DMS. She was in great anguish and Gandhi wrote her a series of letters to console her.

She left for Denmark at the suggestion of her father in May 1920, after a visit to Gandhi. Mr. Menon, now a doctor, visited Gandhi and went to Denmark in 1921. They married in Denmark, returned in December 1921, and began to assist Miss Petersen at *Seva Mandir* (the national girls' school and *ashram*) she established in Porto Novo (Parangipettai). As Dr. Menon was unable to find a job, Miss Petersen engaged him to supervise the construction of the school.

Dr. Menon decided to adopt the Christian religion and was baptised on June 6, 1924. He was then employed by the Porto Novo Mission as a medical missionary and provided with a small dispensary in Chidambaram, near Porto Novo.

The Menons had two daughters–Nan and Tangai–born in 1923 and 1926.

The climate of India began to affect the health of Miss Faering and her children. All three contracted malaria and Miss Faering also suffered from rheumatism. The family moved to Kotagiri, a hill station in the Nilgiris where the DMS had its summer colony: Dr. Menon helped poor patients and could not earn enough to support the family.

The ill health of Miss Faering and the children and the inability of Dr. Menon to support the family were a serious problem during the rest of their lives and a great disappointment for Mrs. Menon. Her wish to serve India and her hope that her children would become Indian and give their best to India were not fulfilled.

Miss Petersen arranged for the Menon family to go to Denmark in 1927. Dr. Menon went from there to England to study medicine at Birmingham. Mrs. Menon and the children joined him in 1929. The Menons were associated with the Woodbrooke Settlement, a Quaker institution in Birmingham, which Gandhi visited in 1931.

While in Denmark, Mrs. Menon gave a series of three lectures on Gandhi on the Danish radio in 1928. She published a biography of Gandhi in Danish in 1930–*Gandhi: En Karakteristik og Fremstilling* (Gandhi: a Sketch and a Portrayal).

Dr. Menon could not get his diploma in two years as he had hoped; he passed the examination in 1931. He worked in a hospital in Birmingham for two more years.

The travel of the Menons to Europe and the costs of Dr. Menon's studies were a heavy burden on the scarce resources of the Porto Novo mission.

The Menons returned to India in February 1934. Dr. Menon looked for a job and after several months found employment at a government hospital in Tanjore (now Thanjavur). But the climate did not suit Mrs. Menon and the children and they had to move to a hill station in February 1935. They had a hard time with frequent illnesses. The long periods of separation of the children from their father were a great strain on the family. Dr. Menon earned little and had to continue to obtain funds from Danish contributions to the school in Porto Novo. He worked as a military doctor during the Second World War, and then returned to work in hospitals in South India.

Mrs. Menon was forced to return to Denmark with her children in the 1950s because of ill health. To quote Kaj Baago:

> "When she died in the autumn of 1962 she was all but forgotten, although the *Porto Novo Mission Journal* published a brief obituary, which described her love for India and her uprightness and courage when in her youth she became faced with the choice between the Missionary Society and the Indian National Movement. The obituary attempted to give a short account of her life, and perhaps it achieved its aim most precisely with these words: 'Her life's course was heroic and tragic to an extent that few have experienced.'"

Navajivan Publishing House, established by Gandhi, in a book entitled "My Dear Child", published about 130 letters from Gandhi in her possession in 1956. The collection below includes some additional letters by Gandhi from the *Collected Works of Mahatma Gandhi* and other sources, as well as letters by Miss Faering to Gandhi, mostly from the Gandhi Archives in Ahmedabad.

For further information, please see:

M.K. Gandhi, *My Dear Child*. Ahmedabad: Navajivan, 1956.

Kaj Baagø, "Mahatma Gandhi's Dear Child" in Frede Højgaard (ed.) *Friends of Gandhi: Inter-war Scandinavian Responses to the Mahatma* (NIAS Report No. 7, 1991).

Kaj Baagø, "Mahatma Gandhis kære barn" in Kikka Mølgaard (ed.) Indien-*Danmark: For-bindelser og Samarbejde*, (Copenhagen, 1983), pages 54-71.

Esther Menon, *Gandhi: En Karakteristik og Fremstilling af de sidste Dages Begivenheder*. Copenhagen: Forord af Jens Rosenkjær, 1930.

Correspondence with Gandhi

Gandhi to Miss Faering, January 11, 1917[25]

Ahmedabad,
January 11, 1917

Dear Esther,

I was delighted to have your note from Bombay.[26] I assure you that we miss you both very much. You were hardly guests to us; you had become members of the family. Hope Miss Petersen is quite herself again. I redirected a batch of letters yesterday and am doing likewise today.

With regards to both of you,

Yours sincerely,
M. K. Gandhi

Gandhi to Miss Faering, January 15, 1917[27]

Ahmedabad,
January 15, 1917

Dear Esther,

I was pleased to receive your nice letter and hear that Miss Petersen had thrown off her cold entirely.

I am glad you found peace in the *ashram*. Yes, both of you we regard as members of the family. You will come whenever you wish to and can.

25. *My Dear Child*, page 3; *Collected Works*, Volume 13, page 327.
26. The note is not available. Miss Faering and Miss Petersen arrived at the *ashram* on January 6, 1917. This note must have been sent soon after they left. Bombay has now been renamed "Mumbai".
27. *My Dear Child*, pages 3-4; *Collected Works*, Volume 13, page 329.

Ramdas[28] is a noble boy. He is the one going to South Africa.[29] I feel sure that he will give a good account of himself there. By way of preparation he has been attending a printing press here, practising at the compositor's desk.

I have learnt enough of you to know that you will put your whole heart into your studies and soon be talking enough Tamil for your purpose.

Pray keep the rules[30] as long as you like. There is no occasion to hurry over sending them.

With kind regards,

Yours,
M. K. Gandhi

Gandhi to Miss Faering, March 20, 1917[31]

Ahmedabad,
March 20, 1917

Dear Esther,

I have an English lady friend[32] and her sister's children who during the hot weather are to live at some hillside place. You are

28. Gandhi's third son.
29. Manilal Gandhi and Ramdas Gandhi, the second and third sons of Gandhi, went to South Africa early in 1917 to serve the Indian community. They helped publish *Indian Opinion*, a weekly founded by Gandhi in 1903.
30. "Draft Constitution for the *Ashram*" containing rules drawn up for the inmates of the *ashram* in 1915. *Collected Works*, Volume 13, pages 91-98.
31. *My Dear Child*, pages 4-5; *Collected Works*, Volume 13, pages 357-58.
32. Miss Cecilia Graham, sister-in-law of H.S.L. Polak, a close associate of Gandhi in South Africa. Mr. and Mrs. Polak were in India in 1917 and helped in the campaign to prohibit export of indentured labour from India.

going to some such place. Could you befriend them if they went to the same station as you? Of course they will bear their own expenses. The thing wanted is good companionship. And I thought of you. If you will befriend them, will you please tell me where you would go, when you would leave, where you would stay and whether they could reside and board at the same place as you will? You will also please give me an idea of the expenses there. You have heard of Mr. Polak. The friend is his sister-in-law. While Mr. and Mrs. Polak travel on public business, they are anxious to locate their children in some hillside place where Mr. Polak's sister-in-law could find suitable company. She is a stranger to India.

With much love from us all,

Yours sincerely,
M. K. Gandhi

The Polaks leave Ahmedabad probably on Monday. I would like you please therefore to wire to me. If you will address

Gandhi,
Ahmedabad,
the wire will reach me.

M. K. G.

Gandhi to Miss Faering, March 31, 1917[33]

Ahmedabad,
March 31, 1917

Dear Esther,

I am putting you to a lot of trouble on behalf of Mrs. Polak's sister. But you have chosen the privilege of letting me be your brother. And I have the credit for being most exacting of those who are nearest and dearest to me. Having made the choice, you must be content to suffer.

33. *My Dear Child*, page 5; *Collected Works*, Volume 13, page 360.

Miss Graham, that is the sister's name, may be able at once to go to Ooty.[34] It is necessary for her and young Polak to be on a hillside without delay. I much fear that I shall not be able to go to Madras in April. If I am able to do so at all this year, it will be after your descent from the hills.

With love to you and Miss Petersen from us all,

Yours sincerely,
M. K. Gandhi

Gandhi to Miss Faering, April 15, 1917[35]

[Gandhi went to Champaran district in Bihar on April 15, 1917, to investigate the condition of peasants being cruelly exploited by indigo planters, who were mostly British.]

Motihari,
Champaran
April 15, 1917

Dear Esther,

Your sweet letter has followed me all the way here. I am almost at the base of the Himalayas. I am studying the condition of the people working under the indigo planters. My work is most difficult. My trust is in God. We can but work and then be careful for nothing.

Pray do not worry about Miss Graham. She has been fixed up at Ooty.

You may address me as *Bapu*[36] if you like. It means father. In the *ashram* it has become a term of endearment. I value your

34. Ootacamund (now renamed Udagamandalam), a hill station in South India. Gandhi sent Miss Graham there on April 6 with one of the inmates of the *ashram*.
35. *My Dear Child*, page 6; *Collected Works*, Volume 13, page 364.
36. *Bapu* (*bapuji, bapujee*) means father. Members of the *ashram* addressed Gandhi as *bapu*.

affection very much indeed. You may continue to use the Ahmedabad address.

With love,
Yours sincerely,
M. K. G.

Gandhi to Miss Faering, April 17, 1917[37]

[The government served notice on Gandhi ordering him to leave the Champaran district. He defied the order and was charged before Court on 18 April. He pleaded guilty, but on April 21, the government withdrew the case and instructed its officials to assist Gandhi.

On June 10, the Bihar government appointed a committee to inquire into all disputes and appointed Gandhi as one of the members. The committee submitted a unanimous report and in November the government enacted the Champaran Agrarian Bill to remove the main grievances.

Motihari was the headquarters of Champaran district and Bettiah a town in the district.]

Motihari,
April 17, 1917

My dear Esther,

I know you will want me to tell you that I am about to be imprisoned. I have come here to remove some labour grievances. The authorities do not want me. Hence the impending imprisonment. Do ask Mr. M. at the *ashram* to send you some papers, and you will know. I am absolutely joyed to think that I shall be imprisoned for the sake of conscience.

Yours
(if you want me to sign)
Bapu

37. *My Dear Child*, pages 6-7; *Collected Works*, Volume 13, page 371.

Gandhi to Miss Faering, May 2, 1917[38]

Motihari,
Champaran,
May 2, 1917

Dear Esther,

I have just received your letter from Ahmedabad. To say "I thank you" would be in your case an empty form. Your interest is much deeper. My experiences here give the greatest joy. The suffering I see around me gives me equal pain. I know that you feel for me because you would like to be in the thick of it all yourself. But your work is cut out for you. For those who are at a distance from you, you can but pray. And that you are doing with all your heart.

I may not be able to leave this place for six months. One of these days, I shall describe to you the nature of the work I am doing here.

Do please go to the *ashram* whenever you can. It is one of your homes if one may have more than one.

You may write to me at the address given at the top.

With love,
Yours,
Bapu

Gandhi to Miss Faering, May 13, 1917[39]

Bettiah,
May 13, 1917

My dear Esther,

Pray do not apologise for writing to me. Your letters are most welcome.

38. *My Dear Child,* page 7; *Collected Works,* Volume 13, page 381.
39. *My Dear Child,* page 9; *Collected Works,* Volume 13, pages 384-85.

I am sure that your duty is to fulfil your undertaking with the Mission with all your heart. You can come to the *ashram* only when they relieve you and when you feel in the clearest possible terms that you will come to render the service of humanity in greater fullness. When that time comes, the *ashram* will receive you as one of its own. Meanwhile you are of course always free to go [to] the *ashram* and stay there as long as you like.

At the *ashram*, we are now trying an experiment in education to serve as a pattern. When you go there, I am sure you will like the teaching staff. They are all, I think, good men and sane.

My work here gives me greater and greater joy day by day. The poor *raiyats*[40] delight in simply sitting round me, feeling that they can trust me to do the right thing. I only hope I am worthy of all this love. I constantly see the planters and do not despair of appealing to their sense of justice on behalf of the *raiyats* who have groaned under the weight of oppression all these long years. I shall send you a copy of my representation to the Government. You may not understand some points in it. Do not hesitate to ask me please.

With love,
Yours,
Bapu

Gandhi to Miss Faering, May 19, 1917[41]

Bettiah,
May 19, 1917

My dear Esther,

Your letter does credit to your heart. I really do not need the Rs.[42] 50/- at the present moment. Just now we have more than we need. If you cannot think of using it for any other purpose you can think of, send it to the *ashram* to be kept for an emergency fund.

40. *Raiyat* (*ryot, ryat*) is a peasant or farmer.
41. *My Dear Child*, page 10; *Collected Works*, Volume 13, page 403.
42. Rupees. Rupee is Indian currency.

The *ashram* too has no present need of money. You will not perhaps be surprised to learn that all the pecuniary assistance in my work has come, in a way, in answer to prayer. I have not been obliged to beg, i.e., for conducting the missions I have undertaken. But this is a long story into which I cannot go.

The work here continues as usual.

Do please remember me to Miss Petersen when you write to her and tell her I shall still expect her promised long letter.

With love,
Yours,
Bapu

Miss Faering to Gandhi, May 20, 1917[43]

May 20, 1917

My dear *Bapu*!

Thank you very, very much for your good letter and the interesting, but so sad representation of this great work you now are in the midst of.

I read it with somewhat the same feeling, which I read Mr. Polak's book about the South African problem. One can hardly believe, humanity has become so cruel and wicked. We say, and not without reason, that this war is cruel and hateful in the sight of God, but war is the gathering and summing up in one place and within a limited time all our sins, which has its root in our selfishness and seeking our own profit, honour and power; so this is much more dreadful and cruel to treat the *ryats* in such a way. If I understand your representation right, so have the planters for years slowly killed those poor peoples' physical as well as spiritual life by depriving them in a very unjust way, not only their proper wages, but even their own means. To do their work, they have been reaping when they had not sowed, and they have dealt in a cruel way with those who have been toiling and labouring for

43. SN6357. SN denotes the serial number of the letter in the Gandhi archives collected by *Harijan Ashram* at Sabarmati.

them, and robbed them of every hope and joy and satisfaction in life, regarding their lives less even than their animals.

Have the *ryats* not actually been treated like slaves, and not been allowed to grow their own crops or use their own carts and ploughs?

But how have things come wrong, so far as this, how have the planters been able to force the *ryats* to pay those high rents and p.c.? I am afraid I do not quite understand the first class. Those that have never indigo plantations. All the rest, I do understand; it is so clearly and plainly put forth, but of course, if one stayed in the place and saw it with one's own eyes, one would understand it still better. But I feel, as if the shame of this crime is mine too, and I think their claim for justice has daily gone up before God's face, and so He has called you, *Bapu,* to do this work, because you are willing to suffer for the sake of righteousness.

No wonder, that all those *ryats* love and trust you, and is it not so, that every human heart is craving and longing for love and sympathy and with full right, and poorest amongst the poor is the one who has lost every hope and desire for love and understanding towards and from his fellow men. And when it is so amongst men, we cannot wonder, that God loves us still more; I like what St. James wrote about this, that God is longing with eagerness for everybody amongst us, but, when I hear about this kind of injustice and cruelty, I find it for a moment hard to trust and believe in the infinite love and almighty power, but on the other hand God has given us a free will. We are not men machines, so He cannot force us against our will to turn away from our evil ways, He can only show us this love in many ways, and I feel this love surround me any day, and therefore it is a real pain to know that millions of people suffer and do not know or feel this heavenly father's love and therefore I do feel I am in great debt to you, *Bapu,* because you every day is revealing this love to those who want it.

I am not sentimental, but when I last night had read about this matter, I could not sleep, it kept me awake, and I thought about their sufferings and patience for years, and I feel so little, when I compared myself with those people.

And I am very thankful, because you sent me this copy, I can now follow the work better in my thoughts and prayers, when I know, where the difficulties lie, and I can only pray, that your day by day may get grace and strength to finish this work.

I read with great interest about the educational system you are going to start in the *ashram*, and I shall only be too glad to come and enjoy and learn from it. Are you going to move the *ashram* to the place we went and saw that day, the 6th of January?[44]

I will not do anything in haste, but wait and be patient.

Some time ago, I wrote to Miss Graham. I got her address from the *ashram*, and I hope and expect, she will come to Kotagiri[45] from the first of June. I can get room there, and she wrote, Mr. Polak's eldest son Waldo has been rather ill, so he needs to go to a hill-station, and Ooty is rather too cold a place, and she does not like Ooty. So I shall be glad the day, they are coming up here.

My present *munshi*[46] wants me to learn Sanskrit; but I think, it is too early. My first duty is to learn Tamil, and learn it well, but I do love to hear Sanskrit, it is like music, so he is sometimes reading Sanskrit to me, because I enjoy to hear it, and in my spare moments I am trying to learn to write the letters.

I hope all your family both in Calcutta[47] and S. A.[48] and in the *ashram* are well, and I pray that you may be strong and of good courage, that you may have good success wherever you go and spread hope, joy and light amongst the people you live with and for.

With much love from yours thankful.
Esther

44. The *ashram* was moved later in the year to a site on the banks of Sabarmati River.
45. A hill station in the Nilgris where members of the Danish mission spent the summers.
46. teacher.
47. Now "Kolkata".
48. South Africa.

Gandhi to Miss Faering, May 26, 1917[49]

Bettiah,
May 26, 1917

My dear Esther,

Your letter is so good that I am taking the liberty of sending it to the Polaks[50] to read and then forward it to Ahmedabad. I hope you don't mind my having taken the liberty.

Those who do not grow indigo, also want to make illegal gains. Hence they force the *raiyat* on their land to labour for them at a trifling wage or none at all at times and make them pay extras apart from rents. Yes, the condition is no better than that of slaves. The further papers I have sent you will throw more light on the question. I must say that the planters are not alone to blame. The planters happen to be English. Indian landlords are not better and some of them are much worse. It is undoubtedly the ignorance on this point of public men that has permitted the wrong to continue so long. Governments rarely move except under pressure.

For you no doubt Tamil[51] takes precedence of every other language. But it will be most helpful if you could master the *Devanagari* script[52]. It is easy and it is the most perfect alphabet in the world in that each letter represents only one sound and almost all the sounds are represented by it.

Yours,
Bapu

[Gandhi sent Miss Faering's letter to Mrs. Millie Graham Polak on May 26 and wrote: "I do hope that

49. *My Dear Child,* pages 10-11; *Collected Works*, Volume 13, pages 418-19.
50. H.S.L. Polak and Mrs. Millie Graham Polak were close associates of Gandhi in South Africa. They were in India in 1917.
51. Tamil is the language of the region in south India where Miss Faering was working.
52. The Sanskrit script used in Hindi and other languages.

Kotagiri is near enough for Cecilia to meet Miss Faering. She is a most kind-hearted girl. Do write to her if you feel inclined. Miss Esther Faering, Spring Cottage, Kotagiri". Kotagiri, where Miss Faering was staying, is in the same district as Ootacamund where Miss Graham was.]

Gandhi to Miss Faering, June 9, 1917[53]

[Miss Faering asked if Europeans did more harm than good to India.]

Bettiah,
June 9, 1917

My dear Esther,

As you will have seen from the papers sent to you, I have been to Ranchi, from which place I returned only yesterday to find your letters.

Yours is a difficult question to answer. The total effect of European activity has not been for the good of India. The general body of Europeans who have come to India have succumbed to the vices of the East instead of imposing their own virtues on the East. It could not well be otherwise. Religion has not made a lasting impression on them, as we see demonstrated even by the present war. My theory is that modern civilisation is decidedly anti-Christian. And what Europeans have brought to India is that civilisation, not the life of Jesus. You and a handful of others are striving to represent that life. It is bound to leave its mark upon the soil. But it must take time. "The mills of God grind slowly". You and people like you are not affected by the evil that stares you in the face. You get behind it, discover the good lying underneath and add it to your own stock, thus producing a perfect blend. What I want is a reciprocity of that method. And so I welcomed your visit to the *ashram*, as I welcome that of many European

53. *My Dear Child*, pages 11-13; *Collected Works*, Volume 13, pages 439-40.

friends who are true to their best traditions and are broadminded enough to take in the best that this land has to give. Have I made myself clear? Please discuss this further and freely with me.

I am likely to serve on the Committee the Government are about to appoint. I am presently framing a general note which will give you the details of the visit to Ranchi.[54] It was a good thing I went.

Mrs. Gandhi and Devdas[55] are here now and so is Polak. Had I been arrested, Mrs. Gandhi and Devdas would have worked among the poor *raiyats* and heartened them for the struggle. I am most anxious for you to meet Mrs. Gandhi at the earliest moment.

Please don't think that I am killing myself with work.

With love from us all,

Yours,
Bapu

Gandhi to Miss Faering, June 11, 1917[56]

Motihari,
June 11, 1917

My dear Esther,

I am here for a day. I received your booklet[57] as I was going to the station. It put me in mind of some of the happiest hours I used to have years ago in South Africa. I read the booklet years ago when I found myself in the company of some very dear Christian friends. I have read it again today with better appreciation if one may write in this manner of a sacred work like this. For me truth

54. Gandhi visited Ranchi for discussions with the Lieutenant-Governor of Bihar, which led to the setting up of a committee to investigate the grievances of the peasants.
55. Devdas (or Devadas) Gandhi, youngest son of Gandhi.
56. *My Dear Child*, pages 13-14; *Collected Works*, Volume 13, page 442.
57. Corinthians, XIII.

and love are interchangeable terms. You may not know that the Gujarati for passive resistance is truth-force. I have variously defined it as truth-force, love-force or soul-force. But truly there is nothing in words. What one has to do is to live a life of love in the midst of the hate we see everywhere. And we cannot do it without unconquerable faith in its efficacy. A great queen named Mirabai lived two or three hundred years ago. She forsook her husband and everything and lived a life of absolute love. Her husband at last became her devotee. We often sing in the *ashram* some fine hymns composed by her. You shall hear and one of these days sing them when you come to the *ashram*.

Thank you for the precious gift. I need such thoughts as are contained in the work.

With love,
Yours,
Bapu

PS.

I am going to follow Drummond's prescription[58] to read the verses on Love daily for three months.

Gandhi to Miss Faering, June 17, 1917[59]

Motihari,
June 17, 1917

My dear Esther,

I am going to Ahmedabad for 4 days. I return on the 28th instant at the latest. There is no secret about what I have and you have every right to ask. My faith in Truth and Love is as vivid as in the fact that I am writing this to you. To me they are convertible terms. Truth and Love conquer all.

Yours sincerely,
Bapu

58. *The Greatest Thing in the World* by Henry Drummond.
59. *My Dear Child,* page 14; *Collected Works,* Volume 13, page 446.

Miss Faering to Gandhi, June 22, 1917[60]

My dear *Bapu,*

In the last night in my old year,[61] I got your letter, and I wish that love and truth may become very real factors in my New Year. And today, when I look back on the past year, my heart is filled with thanks for God's manyfold gifts to me, but most of all I thank Him, because He sent me to the *ashram*; amongst all the gifts and joys the past year brought me, this is the greatest, and next to God I thank you *Bapu* for all, what it means to me, that I may have a home and find friends in the *ashram*.

Last night, when I had a great sorrow my friend Miss Elise (we have been together nearly always) said: "I do wish I could make you happy and see you glad tomorrow on your birthday, and I really know only one way to make you glad, and that is, if I could send you to the *ashram*, and that is impossible". Will those few lines shall only tell, that I do share the *ashram*'s joy in having you back, even it is only for a short time, may it be a time of rest and joy and give strength for the coming work.[62]

With love to all from
Yours thankful Esther

Gandhi to Miss Faering, June 30, 1917[63]

Motihari,
June 30, 1917

My dear Esther,

I have your two letters before me. I returned from Ahmedabad on the 28th. I had a nice time there.

60. SN6363.
61. June 22 was the birthday of Miss Faering.
62. Gandhi was at that time leading a *satyagraha* of peasants in Champaran and returned to the *ashram* for a few days.
63. *My Dear Child*, pages 14-15; *Collected Works*, Volume 13, pages 451-52.

The city life I have always found to be chilling; the village life, free, invigorating and godly.

"Why has God given us so many gifts, powers, skill to invent if we are not to use them?" You have asked a question which I have asked myself and thousands are always asking. My humble opinion is that God has placed temptations in our way, the strength of which is the same as that of the possibilities of rise in moral grandeur. We may use our inventive faculty either for inward growth or for outward indulgence. I may devote my talents for utilising the falls from the Himalayas; I only increase mankind's facilities for indulgence. I may use my talents for discovering laws which govern the falls from the Himalayas within me; I serve myself and mankind by adding to the permanent happiness. You will make up for yourself countless illustrations showing that all our talents are to be utilised only for inward growth which can come from self-restraint alone.

Do please remember me to Mr. Bittmann[64] and thank him on my behalf for permitting you to come to the *ashram* whenever you are free.

Your experience of the young man is nothing extraordinary. Pray do not be impatient to reform men and women whom you meet. The first and the last thing we have to attend to is to reform ourselves. In trying to reform, we seem to be judging. These young men often become worse for our handling. The safest course is to let such men leave us when they are found wanting. I have not sufficiently expressed myself. But you will understand. If not, please ask.

Yours,
Bapu

64. Rev. Johan [John] Edvard Bittmann (1869-1939, a senior member of the Danish Mission in India. He was in India from 1895 to 1936 and lived in Madras (now Chennai). He was understanding and sympathetic to Esther Faering. He visited Gandhi in December 1927 together with Anne Marie Petersen. He joined "Friends of India" in Denmark after retirement.

Gandhi to Miss Faering, July 1, 1917[65]

Motihari,
July 1, 1917

My dear Esther,

I have just received your letter[66] telling you had entered upon a new year, you do not say what year. I appreciate your passion for the *ashram*. May it satisfy all your wants and may it prove a place of joy and peace and of love such as you would find near your parents' hearth. Every year that closes upon us may be so much valuable time gained or lost as we have well or ill used it. To us who want to walk in the fear of God, every added year is added responsibility.

Please tell me what books you are reading for Tamil examination and what you are paying your *munshi*,[67] if you have any.

Yours ever,
Bapu

Letter from Gandhi, July 8, 1917[68]

Ranchi,
July 8, 1917

My dear Esther,

I have come here in connection with the Committee work. I leave here on the 11th for Motihari. This is supposed to be a healthy place being on a plateau.

65. *My Dear Child*, page 16; *Collected Works*, Volume 13, page 454.
66. Her letter of June 22.
67. Teacher.
68. *My Dear Child*, pages 16-17; *Collected Works*, Volume 13, page 466.

Here is a copy of a letter I wrote to *The Pioneer*.[69] I know you will like it. The letter has created quite a stir here. It has been favourably received so far.

Could you send a copy of *The Greatest Thing in the World* to Mr. Polak? I cannot procure it here. I copied out the verses and sent them to him. He now asks for the booklet. The book with me is being used.

Yours,
Bapu

Gandhi to Miss Faering, July 14, 1917[70]

Motihari,
July 14, 1917

My dear Esther,

I have just returned from Ranchi to find your letter awaiting me.

69. "Reply regarding dress to *The Pioneer*", June 30, 1917. *Collected Works*, Volume 13, pages 450-51.
Replying to an article by Mr. Irwin in *The Pioneer* that he was wearing different clothing in Champaran to impress the peasants, Gandhi wrote that he had always worn that dress in India except for a short period:
"The fact is that I wear the national dress because it is the most natural and the most becoming for an Indian. I believe that our copying of the European dress is a sign of our degradation, humiliation and our weakness; and that we are committing a national sin in discarding a dress which is best suited to the Indian climate and which, for its simplicity, art and cheapness, is not to be beaten on the face of the earth and which answers hygienic requirements. Had it not been for a false pride and equally false notions of prestige, Englishmen here would long ago have adopted the Indian costume...."
70. *My Dear Child*, pages 17-18; *Collected Works*, Volume 13, page 472.

You never told me you had taken to vegetarianism. I am sure it is the proper thing for this climate, apart from its religious value. A convert to vegetarianism is often told to eat of pulses, butter, cheese and milk more than during the meat-eating period. This is a mistake. Pulses may be eaten only sparingly. If one takes a fair quantity of milk, very little butter is required.

In my opinion, it is wrong to possess unnecessary things; they presuppose defence of things possessed against those who may covet them. They require care and attention which might well be devoted to more important matters and loss of them always leaves a pang, no matter how detached you may feel about them.

The sittings of the Committee commence on Monday.

I was delighted to see your thoughtful gifts to Mrs. Gandhi.

With love from us all,

Yours,
Bapu

Gandhi to Miss Faering, August 3, 1917[71]

Nadiad,
August 3, 1917

My dear Esther,

You have raised big questions. I think the command of Jesus is unequivocal. All killing is bad for one who is filled with love. He will not need to kill. He will not kill. He who is filled with pity for the snake and does not fear him will not kill him and the snake will not hurt him. This state of innocence is the one we must reach. But only a few can reach it. It seems to me to be impossible for nations to reach it. Equal progress in all is an inconceivable situation. Nations will therefore always fight. One of them will be

71. *My Dear Child*, pages 18-19; *Collected Works*, Volume 13, pages 485-86.

less wrong than the other. A nation to be in the right can only fight with soul-force. Such a nation has still to be born. I had hoped that India was that nation. I fear I was wrong. The utmost I expect of India is that she may become a great restraining force. But she must acquire the ability to fight and suffer before she can speak to the world with any degree of effect.

The pertinent question for you and me is what is our duty as individuals. I have come to this workable decision for myself, "I will not kill anyone for any cause whatsoever but be killed by him if resistance or his will render my being killed necessary". I would give similar advice to everybody. But where I know that there is want of will altogether, I would advise him to exert his will and fight. There is no love where there is no will. In India there is not only no love but hatred due to emasculation. There is the strongest desire to fight and kill side by side with utter helplessness. This desire must be satisfied by restoring the capacity for fighting.[72] Then comes the choice.

Yes, the very act of forgiving and loving shows superiority in the doer. But that way of putting the proposition begs the question, who can love? A mouse as mouse cannot love a cat. A mouse cannot be commonly said to refrain from hurting a cat. You do not love him whom you fear. Immediately you cease to fear, you are ready for your choice-to strike or to refrain. To refrain is proof of awakening of the soul in man; to strike is proof of body-force. The ability to strike must be present when the power of the soul is demonstrated. This does not mean that we must be bodily superior to the adversary.

This is not a satisfactory letter but I think you will follow my argument. But in matters such as these, prayer is the thing.

With love

72. Gandhi had at the time retained faith in the British Empire, and encouraged recruitment of Indian soldiers during the First World War. He became an absolute pacifist in later years.

Gandhi to Miss Faering, August 12, 1917[73]

Bettiah,
August 12, 1917

My dear Esther,

I have a moment to spare today. The lines you send are good and true. Belief and hope are great. They are indispensable for success. But love is greater. I find here that too great a strain is put upon it. Only this morning a powerfully built man came to me and insisted on my giving him help which was not in my power to give him. He would not leave me. I begged of him. He began weeping and beating his breast. His case is nothing. He came out of hope and love. How would I, wanting to love him, treat him? Assuming that his weeping was sincere, must I put up with his presence and go on talking to him? Such problems arise every day. Love has to be patient. How to apply the injunction in cases such as I have quoted? The only safe guide is the monitor within if one is pure-minded and sure of one's sincerity. We often deceive ourselves.

You may write for the time being to Ahmedabad which I expect to reach within a week from now. The Committee will have finished its deliberations within 3 days from today.

What treatment did you receive when you had the snake bite? How did you manage to get bitten? Where did it bite you? Was the snake caught and killed? I am always interested in the question of snake-bites and snakes.

With love from us all,

Yours,
Bapu

73. *My Dear Child*, page 20; *Collected Works*, Volume 13, page 499.

Gandhi to Miss Faering, September 5, 1917[74]

Ahmedabad,
September 5, 1917

My dear Esther,

I have your two letters really to answer, the last one is most touching. The cause of the terrible pain I have suffered was within myself. I twice ate when I ought not to have. The result was dysentery in a most acute form. I am now much better and am making daily progress. In four or five days, I shall be out of bed.

With love,
Bapu

Gandhi to Miss Faering, September 6, 1917[75]

Ahmedabad,
September 6, 1917

My dear Esther,

I was delighted to receive your note. I hope to be in Madras for a day only on the 14th instant. I shall have to leave on the 15th instant in the evening.

Ever since my arrival here, I have been on the move trying to spread the gospel of *Satyagraha*[76] in the place of methods of violence. It is an uphill task. You will see from the enclosed what I mean by *Satyagraha*.

74. *My Dear Child*, page 21; *Collected Works*, Volume 13, page 526.
75. *My Dear Child*, pages 21-22; *Collected Works*, Volume 13, pages 526-27.
76. Literally "truth force", term used by Gandhi for non-violent resistance.

It was not my intention that your remarks upon dress should be published. I forgot to warn Dr. M. about it. He liked your views so much that he could not restrain himself. I do hope you don't mind my sending to Dr. M. such of your letters as may appear to be helpful.

"To be free from desire" is a technical expression and means desire to be or possess something short of the highest. Thus, love of God is not "a desire". It is the natural longing. But to possess a fortune so that I may do good is a desire and therefore to be curbed. Our good acts must be as natural to us as the twinkling of our eyes. Without our desiring, they act automatically. The doing of good should be just as natural to us.

Yours ever,
Bapu

Gandhi to Miss Faering, October 4, 1917[77]

Ranchi,
October 4, 1917

Dear Esther,

I have not been able to write to you as often as I should like to have. I must let you share one of the richest experiences of life. Contrary to my expectation and owing to great strain, I was down with malaria, just when I could least afford to have illness. I had to attend the Committee work every day. Quinine was the drug prescribed. I would not take it. My faith has saved me. I missed not a single meeting and we signed an unanimous report yesterday.[78] I believe I have seen the last of the illness too. I have

77. *My Dear Child*, pages 22-23; *Collected Works*, Volume 13, page 562.
78. Report of the Champaran Agrarian Enquiry Committee. *Collected Works*, Volume 13, Appendix XI.

not the time to go into greater detail but when we meet you should ask me to give you the details of this experience. I take it you have read my letter to the Press on the railways.[79] If you have missed it, you should ask the *ashram* to let you have a copy.

You were quite right [in] not coming to Madras.[80] Love must be patient and humble. It is the rich and leisurely who can afford to be demonstrative in their love. We humble folks have naturally a different and better method of showing love. True love acts when it must, meanwhile it daily grows silently but steadily. In Motihari from 7th to 13th. Then Ahmedabad.

Yours,
Bapu

Gandhi to Miss Faering, December 12, 1917[81]

Motihari,
Champaran,
December 12, 1917

Dear Esther,

Your letter just received grieves me. "Be careful for nothing" comes to my lips as I write these lines. Why fret and worry? You are just now passing through fire.[82] I am sure you will come out

79. "Letter to the Press on Third Class Travelling on Indian Railways", September 25, 1917. *Collected Works*, Volume 13, pages 547-51.
Gandhi, who travelled in third class, drew attention to the overcrowding and filth in the third class compartments and to corruption in the railways.
80. Gandhi was in Madras only for a few hours on September 14-15.
81. *My Dear Child*, pages 23-24; *Collected Works*, Volume 14, pages 106-07.
82. She was yearning to visit Gandhi's *ashram*, but the Danish Mission authorities had refused her permission to spend the Christmas holidays there.

unhurt. It is your clear duty just now to obey those to whom you have given the right to control your movements.[83] You can oppose them only when they clearly hinder your spiritual progress. They receive the benefit of any doubt. You could certainly reason with them that just at this time of the year you will have perfect weather in Ahmedabad, loving attention and no worry. The very change of surroundings is likely to do you good. If you still fail, you have to accept their opposition with resignation. Please do not worry over your exam. That is a mere nothing. We are best tried when we are thwarted in what to us are holy purposes. God's ways are strange and inscrutable. Not our will but His must be our Law.

Please write to me frequently and, up to the end of the year, send your letters to Motihari. I should even value a telegram saying you are at peace with yourself, if you are that when you receive this.

With love,

Yours,
Bapu

Gandhi to Miss Faering, January 13, 1918[84]

Motihari,
January 13, 1918

My dear Esther,

Having been wandering about, I have not been able to reply to your letters. I was in Calcutta, thence went to Bombay and the *ashram* and returned only yesterday. I had varied experiences which I cannot describe for want of time.

83. that is, the Danish Missionary Society.
84. *My Dear Child*, pages 24-25; *Collected Works*, Volume 14, page 146.

To say that perfection is not attainable on this earth is to deny God. The statement about impossibility of ridding ourselves of sin clearly refers to a stage in life. But we need not search scriptures in support of the assertion. We do see men constantly becoming better under effort and discipline. There is no occasion for limiting the capacity for improvement. Life to me would lose all its interest if I feel that I *could* not attain perfect love on earth. After all, what matters is that our capacity for loving ever expands. It is a slow process. How shall you love the men who thwart you even in well-doing? And yet that is the time of supreme test.

I hope that you are now enjoying greater peace of mind. Let your love for the *ashram* be a source of strength in your attempt to do your duty there.[85] The *ashram* is undoubtedly intended to teach us to do our assigned task with the utmost attention and with cheerfulness. There is meaning in our wishes (however pure) not being fulfilled. Not our will but His will be done.

I hope you are making progress in your Tamil lessons.

Did you receive from Messrs Natesan & Co.[86] a book they have brought out containing my speeches and writings? I am sending you a copy of my speech in Calcutta on Social Service.[87]

With love.

Yours,
Bapu

85. Miss Faering was at the time teaching at the Danish Mission Boarding School at Tirukoilur, near Madras.
86. publishers in Madras.
87. "Address at All-India Social Service Conference", December 31, 1917. *Collected Works*, Volume 14, pages 121-28.

Gandhi to Miss Faering, April 2, 1918[88]

April 2, 1918

My dear child,

I have your letter. The Poet[89] has now arrived here. That keeps me busy. He inquired about you.[90] There is going to be a big strike on in Ahmedabad.[91] I don't know where it will lead to. It may keep me busy for some time. When are you likely now to go home? It is a good thing you are at Kotagiri. I can understand your inability to write real letters. There are things in life for which there is no remedy but time. We have only to allow nature to perform the healing process.

With love,

Yours ever,
Bapu

Gandhi to Miss Faering, April 8, 1918[92]

On the train,
April 8, 1918

Dear Esther,

I seem to have been cruelly neglectful in my correspondence with you. I could not be satisfied with giving only a line to you. I

88. *My Dear Child*, page 26.
89. Poet Rabindranath Tagore visited Ahmedabad.
90. Miss Faering and Miss Petersen had visited Santiniketan, the school established by Tagore at Bolpur in Bengal, during their tour of schools in 1917.
91. A strike of workers in the textile mills.
92. *My Dear Child*, pages 26-27; *Collected Works*, Volume 14, pages 316-17.

wanted to give you a long love-letter. I have not the quiet for framing such a letter. And I dare not wait any longer.

I do not know how I can describe my activities not one of which is of my own seeking. They have all come to me with a persistence I dare not oppose. What is a soldier to do if he is hemmed in on all sides? Is he to concentrate his effort on dealing with one attack only and to court extinction by ignoring the other attacks that are being simultaneously delivered? Obviously safety lies in dealing with all in the best way he can. Such is almost my position. Distress pleads before me from all sides. I dare not refuse help where I know the remedy.[93]

The Ahmedabad strike provided the richest lessons of life. The power of love was never so effectively demonstrated to me as it was during the lock-out. The existence of God was realised by the mass of men before me as soon as the fast was declared. Your telegram was the most-touching and the truest of all. Those four days were to me days of peace, blessing and spiritual uplifting. There never was the slightest desire to eat during those days.[94]

93. The reference is to requests he received from peasants in Champaran and Kaira, and workers in Ahmedabad, for guidance to enable them to secure redress of their grievances.
94. Workers in Ahmedabad textile mills struck work for an increase in bonus and were locked out. Gandhi, who had participated in discussions between mill owners and workers, guided the workers during the strike. The workers took a vow not to go back to work unless they received a 35 percent bonus, which Gandhi had recommended as a compromise between the 70 percent they received earlier and the 20 percent offered by the employers. The strike dragged on as the mill owners refused to budge from their offer and rejected arbitration. On March 15, 1918, when the strikers seemed to be weakening, he announced to the workers: "Unless the strikers rally and continue the strike till a settlement is reached, or till they leave the mills altogether, I will not touch any food". He broke the fast on April 18 when a settlement was reached, with the mill owners agreeing to a 35 per cent bonus.

The Kaira affair you must have understood from my letter to the Press.[95] I wrote one on the fast too.[96] If you have not seen the letters, please let me know.

I hope you are keeping well. In liver complaints nothing answers so well as fasting.

Please address your letters to Ahmedabad or rather Sabarmati.[97]

With love,

Yours,
Bapu

95. "Statement to the Press on the Kheda Situation", March 28, 1918. *Collected Works*, Volume 14, pages 288-92.
In the district of Kheda (Kaira), there was a widespread failure of the crops in the year 1917-18. Under the Revenue Rules, the cultivators were entitled to a suspension of the land tax. However, revenue collectors made erroneous valuations of the crops and the government provided relief for only a few villages. Gandhi made an extensive survey of the district which proved that the failure was much more extensive. But the government rejected his requests to appoint an impartial committee of inquiry or adopt other measures to alleviate distress. Instead it resorted to coercive measures for the collection of revenue and, on Gandhi's advice, the cultivators refused to pay taxes. Gandhi wrote this letter to obtain public support for their struggle.
Faced with mass resistance, the Government subsequently issued orders to exempt all poor peasants from taxes.
96. "Letter to the Press", March 27, 1918. *Collected Works*, Volume 14, pages 283-86.
Gandhi wrote that he was aware that there were serious defects in his vow because his action put undue pressure on the employers whose friendship he enjoyed, "but I preferred the ignominy of having unworthily compromised by my vow the position and independence of the mill owners rather than that it should be said by posterity that 10,000 men [mill workers] had suddenly broken a vow which they had for over twenty days solemnly taken and repeated in the name of God".
97. Gandhi moved his *ashram* from Kocharab to a site on the banks of river Sabarmati, in Ahmedabad, in 1917.

Gandhi to Miss Faering, May 11, 1918[98]

[Sabarmati,]
May 11, 1918

My dear Esther,

I have your letter. I shall-we shall look forward to your coming to the *ashram* during Xmas. The main buildings will then have been ready and the weather will be delightful.

I hope you have read my letter to the Viceroy[99] as also my letter in reply to Mr. Pratt's speech.[100] They contain in the briefest form my views on Government and the philosophy of life, and the one to the Viceroy shows in the vividest form the view I take of the law of love and suffering. Passive Resistance expresses the idea in the crudest form. Indeed, I dislike the phrase as a weapon of the weak. It totally misrepresents the law of love. Love is the epitome of strength. Love flows the freeliest only when there is entire absence of fear. Punishments of the loved ones are like balm to the soul.

Will you not try an absolute fast for your liver? You may drink boiled water copiously and, if that is not enough, you may drink orange juice diluted with water. If you feel weak and faint, lie in bed, better still take a cold hip bath, i.e., sit in a tub with your legs and the upper part of the body out of water. It is most invigorating. There is nothing like fasting for liver complaints.

Yours sincerely,
Bapu

98. *The Diary of Mahadev Desai*; Collected *Works*, Volume 14, page 394.
99. "Letter to Viceroy", suggesting that response to the Indian claim for home rule and respect for Muslim sentiments concerning the rights of Muslim States and the holy places were essential to secure full support for the war effort, April 29, 1918. *Collected Works*, Volume 14, pages 377-79.
100. "Letter to *The Bombay Chronicle*", about the no-tax campaign in the Kheda district, April 15, 1918. *Collected Works*, Volume 14, pages 338-41.

Gandhi to Miss Faering, June 30, 1918[101]

[This was in reply to Esther Faering's question: "How can one, who believes firmly and has given his own life for the sake of exercising passive resistance always and everywhere, ask others to join the war and fight ?"]

Nadiad,
June 30, 1918

My dear Esther,

I had no time to write to you ere this. I wonder if you have read all I have been writing and saying just now. What am I to advise a man to do who wants to kill but is unable owing to his being maimed? Before I can make him feel the virtue of not killing, I must restore to him the arm he has lost. I have always advised young Indians to join the army, but have hitherto refrained from actively asking them to do so, because I did not feel sufficiently interested in the purely political life of the country or in the war itself. But a different and difficult situation faced me in Delhi. I felt at once that I was playing with the greatest problem of life in not tackling the question of joining the army seriously. Either we must renounce the benefits of the State or help it to the best of our ability to prosecute the war. We are not ready to renounce. Indians have a double duty to perform. If they are to preach the mission of peace, they must first prove their ability in war.

This is a terrible discovery but it is true. A nation that is unfit to fight cannot from experience prove the virtue of not fighting. I do not infer from this that India must fight. But I do say that India must know how to fight. *Ahimsa* is the eradication of the desire to injure or to kill. *Ahimsa* can be practised only towards those that are inferior to you in every way. It follows therefore that to become a full *ahimsaist* you have to attain absolute perfection. Must we all then first try to become Sandows before we can love perfectly? This seems to be unnecessary. It is enough if we can face the world without flinching. It is personal courage that is an absolute necessity. And some will acquire that courage

101. *My Dear Child*, pages 28-29; *Collected Works*, Volume 14, pages 462-63.

only after they have been trained to fight. I know I have put the argument most clumsily. I am passing through new experiences. I am struggling to express myself. Some things are still obscure to me.

And I am trying to find words for others which are plain to me. I am praying for light and guidance and am acting with the greatest deliberation. Do please write and fight every inch of the ground that to you may appear untenable. That will enable me to find the way.

With love,

Yours,
Bapu

[PS.]

Devdas is in Madras now and, if you are in Madras, you should meet him. His address is.... He is taking Hindi classes.

Gandhi to Miss Faering, July 9, 1918[102]

Nadiad,
July 9, 1918

My dear sister,

Of course you were quite right in putting me the question you did. I am looking forward to your reply to my explanation.

I appreciate your preference for country life and country children. They are more innocent and hence more loveable.

Yes, it is your duty to continue your work to the end of your contract.[103] I know the girls[104] will gain by your very contact. And for that matter I don't mind their receiving faulty education.

102. *My Dear Child*, pages 29-30; *Collected Works*, Volume 14, page 478.
103. Contract with the Danish Missionary Society (DMS).
104. Pupils in the Danish Mission Boarding School, Tirukoilur.

Devdas has just risen from a sick-bed. I know he will be delighted to meet you. Do please find him out, if he has not found you out. And if you have the time, I would like you to meet him as often as possible.

With love,

Yours,
Bapu

Gandhi to Miss Faering, July 22, 1918[105]

Bombay,
July 22, 1918

My dear child,

I have been debating with myself whether to write to you or not to. Your letter made painful reading. I am today at the *ashram* and have just worn the second vest sent by you. I came to know of it only today. It does not fit well. The sleeves are too short. But that matters little. I am wearing it and shall wear it out.

I am quite sure that you must quietly go through your contract even though you may be prohibited from coming to the *ashram* or writing to me. You will gain greater strength of will and purpose by the enforced discipline and restraint.

It will be a privilege if you are permitted to write to me and receive letters. Do please tell me what final decision has been arrived at.

I have suspended Civil Disobedience for the time being. You will see my letter to the Press.

With love,

Yours,
Bapu

105. *My Dear Child*, pages 30-31; *Collected Works*, Volume 14, page 497.

Gandhi to Miss Faering, undated, 1918[106]

Bombay,
1918

My dear Esther,

This is my first attempt to write after the relapse.[107]

Though I am not quite clear about your course of duty, I suppose it is as well that you responded to Mr. Andrews' appeal.[108] I myself doubt the utility of your going there. Your letters to follow will make this point clear. I am very, very sorry that you are not at the *ashram*, during this long vacation. The enforced separation however brings you closer to the *ashram*.

You will be glad to hear that I daily wear the vests made by you. They are a perpetual reminder of your long service.

I am feeling better for the last two days but no progress like this can be considered reliable until it lasts a fortnight or so.

More from Mahadev.[109]

With love,

Yours,
Bapu

[Gandhi wrote to C.F. Andrews on January 6, 1919:

"So far as my convenience is concerned your having sent Miss Faering to Bolpur was all right. But I did consider your

106. *My Dear Child*, page 31; *Collected Works*, Volume 15, pages 68-69.
107. Gandhi suffered from dysentery in August 1918. He was ill for more than two months.
108. C.F. Andrews suggested that Esther Faering go and work at Santiniketan, the school established by Poet Rabindranath Tagore in Bolpur, Bengal, where he was working.
109. Mahadev Desai, secretary to Gandhi.

action impulsive. As you assure me that she entirely filled your place I can have nothing more to say. But I felt upon Miss Faering's letter that she could not very well take the higher English classes, or for that matter, even the lower classes at Santiniketan.[110] I suppose there is nothing insur-mountable for one possessing the faith that Miss Faering does abundantly and she has succeeded where thousands would have failed. Has she taken her discharge from the Danish Mission, because you talk of her coming to me after her finishing Bolpur? If she has got her discharge without causing any bad feeling, it is a great thing...".[111]]

Gandhi to Miss Faering, January 25, 1919[112]

[This was in reply to a letter in which Miss Faering asked: "Do we take a vow in order to help and strengthen our character? Does God require us to take any kind of vows? Can a vow not become fatal? I do ask you *Bapu* in all reverence because I desire to get more light over this question. I believe that God suffers because you now are suffering, *Bapu*, although you suffer with joy. But if God is a father, and if God is perfect love, does it not then cause suffering to Him when His children take burden upon them, which they are not asked to carry? If you could explain [to] me the deeper meaning of the vow it might help me in my own life".

She was perhaps referring to the vow taken by Gandhi some years earlier not to drink milk, because of the cruel way in which

110. Santiniketan was the school established by Rabindranath Tagore in Bolpur.
111. *The Diary of Mahadev Desai*; *Collected Works*, Volume 15, pages 69-70.
112. *The Diary of Mahadev Desai*; *Collected Works*, Volume 15, pages 76-77.

cows were milked in India. In February 1919 when he was very ill, he was persuaded to drink goat's milk.]

Bombay,
January 25, 1919

My dear Esther,

I shall try to answer your very very pertinent question as fully as possible. A vow is nothing but a fixed resolution to do or abstain from doing a particular thing. During the self-denial week, the members of the Salvation Army take a vow to abstain from taking jam or other eatable for a fixed period. During Lent, the Roman Catholics undergo certain privations. That is also a vow. In each case, the result expected is the same, viz., purification and expression of the soul. By these resolutions, you bring the body under subjection. Body is matter, soul is spirit, and there is internal conflict between matter and spirit. Triumph of matter over the spirit means destruction of the latter. It is common knowledge that [this is] in the same proportion that we indulge the body or mortify the soul. Body or matter has undoubtedly its uses. The spirit can express itself only through matter or body. But that result can be obtained only when the body is used as an instrument for the uplifting of the soul. The vast majority of the human families do not use the body in that manner. The result is triumph of the body or matter over the spirit or the soul. We who know the soul to be imperishable living in a body which ever changes its substance and is perishable must by making fixed resolutions bring our bodies under such control that finally we may be able to use them for the fullest service of the soul. This idea is fairly clearly brought out in the New Testament. But I have seen it nowhere explained as fully and clearly as in the Hindu scriptures. You will find this law of self-denial written in every page of the *Ramayana* and the *Mahabharata*. Have you read these two books? If not, you should one of these days read them carefully and with the eye of faith. There is a great deal of fabulous matter about these two books. They are designed for the masses and the authors have deliberately chosen to write them in a manner that would make them acceptable to the people. They have hit upon the easiest method of carrying the truth to the millions, and experience of ages shows that they have been marvelously successful. If I have not made myself sufficiently understood or written convincingly, please tell me so and I shall endeavour again. I have undergone an operation.[113] Today is the sixth day. I do not know whether it is a successful operation. It was performed by an eminent surgeon.

He is undoubtedly a very careful man. It would be no fault of his if I have to continue to suffer pain in spite of the operation.

With love,

Ever yours,
Bapu

Miss Faering to Mahadev Desai, secretary to Gandhi, March 24, 1919[114]

Tirucoilur
March 24, 1919

My dear friend and brother,

I cannot but send you some few lines and tell you that I was deeply touched by your letter because I felt that your kind words are undeserved. As far as I can say, it is true that I love India and feel for India and her people, as if I was one with her and them, and that is my only aim, that I may so learn to love and serve her, so I may gain my birthright to India through love, a child's love to its mother, father and sisters. And in this way may your word inspire and help me, so I by and by can deserve a little of them.

But you do not realise the joy and feeling of thankfulness you gave me, when you wrote that "the Lord Christ had taught me this kind of love".

I have no greater desire than a little of His love may shine forth through me, and He had only one message to bring to this world, namely: God is love-serve Him; God is love-obey Him; God is love–love Him; God is love-be like Him. Can we live up to this

113. Dr. Dalal of Bombay operated Gandhi for piles.
114. SN19812.

message? His is the, He was the living example, so we love him simply because He loved us first. But quite apart from this, that the only commandment Christ gave was: "Love one another"; then it is quite natural for me to love India. When I came to India, I felt at once at home; and here I have found my living ideal, the incarnation of God in man. So next to the great experience when Christ became a living reality in my life, I have no other event for which I am so happy and thankful as the day when I first met *Bapu*; here I found the divine love shining forth clearer than the brightest star; and truth and humanity I found in him as nowhere else, and so I bow down in deepest reverence, love and admiration for true greatness. *Bapu* became for me the manifestation of the love of God and His aim with regard to man, so he came into my life as the living ideal, for which I have been seeking for years. India gave me the very best in life in many ways; shall I then not love her and serve her and sing her praise before other nations?

I am not blind for India's need, but I love her all the more, when I seek to face the truth and at the same time can understand and forgive, and when I know myself, it is so very easy to understand and forgive.

With love to all and yourself

Yours very sincerely
Esther Bahen[115]

Gandhi to Miss Faering, April 1, 1919[116]

Secunderabad,
April 1, 1919

My dear child,

My hand is still too shaky for steady and continuous writing.

115. Sister.
116. *The Diary of Mahadev Desai; Collected Works*, Volume 15, pages 170-71.

But I feel I must make the attempt to give you something in my own hand. I was so sorry I did not see you at the station.[117] I felt keenly for you and poor Mahadev. Both of you are sensitive, almost cast in the same mould. I was shuddering as I looked through the window when the train steamed out. I felt that he would run so madly to catch the train that he might drop down from sheer exhaustion. I was glad to see him at Bezwada.

I hope you wrote to the Collector[118] as you had agreed you would. Please let me know whether he said anything in reply.[119]

Please tell the girls[120] I am going to make daily use of the blanket sheet they have sent me. But I expect them soon to be able to weave hand-spun cotton and spin it themselves. The music of the spinning-wheel is superior to any I know; for it is the music that finally clothes the naked. Even when the machines will be rusting from disuse (for man will some day be sick unto death of the maddening speed of the machines), posterity will still require clothing and hand-spun yarn will be the fashion. I am asking Maganlal[121] to send you some hand-spun yarn.

Our train was late and we missed the connection here. So we have an idle day. This enables me to write to you.

117. In Madras (now "Chennai"). Gandhi was in Madras on March 29-30, and went from there to Bezwada (now "Vijayawada").
118. district officer.
119. Miss Faering decided to seek naturalisation in India.
120. in the Danish Mission Boarding School, where Miss Faering was working.
121. Maganlal Gandhi (1883-1928); second son of Khushalchand, cousin of Mahatma Gandhi. He was for some time manager of the Phoenix Settlement near Durban in South Africa. He was manager of *Satyagraha Ashram*, Sabarmati, from 1915 until his death in 1928.

I wish you could introduce Hindi in your school. You may consult the Superintendent about it. Have you read my plea for Hindi?[122]

With deep love,

Yours,
Bapu

Gandhi to Miss Faering, April 10, 1919[123]

On the way to Bombay under arrest,[124]

April 10, 1919

My dear child,

I have your bank note. I only hope you will not deny yourself the necessaries of life. I am handing the note to the *ashram*. Is that right?

I received last night on my way to Delhi an order not to enter the Punjab. I disobeyed it there and then and I was arrested. I received two further orders-one not to enter the Province of Delhi and the other to confine myself to Bombay. They are now taking me to Bombay. If they set me free I shall immediately disobey the order of confinement. I am perhaps the happiest man on earth today. I have during these two months experienced boundless love. And now I find myself arrested although I bear no ill will to anybody

122. Gandhi was advocating the adoption of Hindi as the national language of India and the propagation of Hindi in non-Hindi speaking areas.
123. *My Dear Child*, page 34; *Collected Works*, Volume 15, pages 209-10.
124. On April 9, when he was organising nation-wide protests against new repressive legislation (the Rowlatt Act), Gandhi was served with orders prohibiting him from entering Delhi or Punjab. He defied the order and was then arrested and taken to Bombay. He was released in Bombay on April 11.

and although I am the one man who can today preserve the peace in India as no other man can.[125] My imprisonment therefore will show the wrongdoer in his nakedness. And he can do me no harm for my spirit remains calm and unruffled.

You will rejoice that you have a friend to whom God has given the power to love even those who call themselves his enemies and to rejoice in sufferings. I say this because I do not want you to grieve over the impending imprisonment. The officer in charge of me is very kind and attentive.

More from Mahadev if he remains free for any length of time.

With love,

Yours ever,
Bapu

[PS.]

Did you receive my letter written in Bezwada or some place on my way to Bombay from Madras?[126]

Bapu

Miss Faering to Mahadev Desai and Gandhi, April 23-24, 1919[127]

To be read by *Bapu*,
April 23, 1919

Dear friend,

Having left Tirukoilur for some few days in order to stay together with a dear friend, a lady doctor, who now is going home to Denmark, because she has got consumption, I was not able to read your letter earlier than yesterday.

125. Repression led to sporadic violent protests and Gandhi was appealing to the people to avoid violence.
126. He sent the letter from Secunderabad on April 10. See above.
127. SN6559.

I think it has been a very hard time not only for *Bapu*, but for all those who love him and are willing to link their lives up together with his.[128] We have all been suffering with him, but this suffering has been 100 times greater and of a more serious..., He had to recognize that our own people, as a whole, is very far from understanding what *satyagraha* really means; it is by no means easy to become a *satyagrahi*; it is only for the spiritual-minded and those who have got complete control over their actions and words or over their body and soul. *Bapu* is an "over-soul" and as you said very like Jesus Christ, and I believe, that such kind of men will never fully be understood by the great masses; they can obtain their worship, admiration and a certain kind of love for a time, but if they are tested they cannot stand the test, as they never have accepted the spiritual law of love in their own private lives. How can we the great masses then expect them all on a ... to obey this most highest law. Am I right?

Bapu himself has got spiritual strength both to fast and carry over this truth-force; and his love to his people is stronger than death and cannot be quenched by many waters, but his suffering now and his disappointment regarding our people must be deeper and greater than you or I can tell, and yet I know he will never give up his faith in the people or in the strength of *satyagraha*–that is against his nature which again and again has been purified and sanctified through vicarious suffering.

We may ask: why should all this come and hinder the true and noble fight for the delibe-ration of the ... I cannot see through the whole matter but I know from my own experience, that whenever we fight most earnestly for all, what is good, pure, true, noble, then at once evil powers and unknown forces will try their utmost in order to destroy the good and righteous efforts; and for a time it may appear to the worldly man, as if darkness and evil is stronger than love and light but we know otherwise. Love and Truth will always conquer at the end and triumph over evil. Therefore was Jesus able to say on the Cross at the darkest time of his life, "It is fulfilled"–because He saw through the veil and

128. Riots broke out after the arrest of Gandhi and martial law was declared in Ahmedabad. He tried to restore peace and on April 13, 1919, undertook a 72-hour penitential fast in Ahmedabad.

saw the ... victory over death and evil, but it was not an easy thing for him to prove that God is Love–and yet holy-and as His wonderful love is able to transform our lives and change our minds, so *Bapu* too has got this power in his own life to illustrate what love means and to send the pure rays or sparks of love into the lives of many poor and downtrodden men, but all this only because he has learnt to give up all, which the common man holds most dear to the ever self-seeking law of ego ... or self. *Bapu* has accepted in his own life the great law in nature, which Jesus once expressed in the following words:

> "Unless the grain of wheat falling into the ground die, itself remaineth alone. But if it die, it bringeth forth much fruit".

And so today *Bapu* is to my mind greater than ever before, because he in the critical moment was able to look quite apart from himself without for a moment to lose faith in this principle based upon love and truth, and only therefore he was able to look at the good of others and so avoid violence and bloodshed. And if anything of this sort has happened in *Bapu's* name, we can know how great and deep his pain and suffering must have been.

But you and I and all who trust and love *Bapu* need not to lose courage but we need to practice the law of love or, if you will, the law of "*ahimsa*" more earnestly in our daily lives. We must learn that it takes a long time to build up a holy pure nation; so let us each and one concentrate our body, soul and spirit for the service of God in this world amidst all those who suffer and sin and ... injustice in so many ways. And I do believe that the time shall come when perfect love and righteousness shall reign everywhere. And we have to live for this great idea and ideal; is it not a glorious aspect of life, yea! Not only shall we live for this idea about God's Kingdom upon earth, but we shall die for it, if we may be called to that highest privilege to die and bear witness for truth.

My dear *Bapu*,

I wrote to Mahadeo[129] that it was not easy to write to you now, as I felt sometimes we have no right to enter into the sacred sorrows of others before we are called for–but for many many days

129. Mahadev (Mahadeo) Desai, secretary to Gandhi.

I have been longing for permission to write to you; and yet I do not know how to write. Who am I that I should possess the right discrimination to speak in this matter; but you have once given me the right to speak to you as I feel. And when I now only can express myself to you through a letter or an answer to V.A. Sundaram[130], I know you will both understand me and forgive me, if you think I am wrong in my views. I was very happy to get your last letter, *Bapu*, dated the 10th of April, the day I ... shall forget in my life.

I am thankful and happy knowing that you will use my gift of love for the *ashram* where I have received such great blessings.

No, *Bapu* I fear I have more than I need for my daily life but you have shown the way of giving, and the more we or I could learn to give the more I should feel happy and free, but there is no joy in giving as long as I only give out of my abundance.

Yes, *Bapu*, amidst all anxiety, I did rejoice when I saw how you actually could love and bless those who did harm unto you. Thus you manifested the Love of God abiding in you.

I send you here the memorial I have written to the Government. I have not yet posted it as I must first hear your advice.

I do not know what is written in the Indian Act of Naturalisation, Act XXX of 1852. I think I ought to know that.

With much love from your
thankful child Esther

April 24, 1919
Tirukoilur

My dear Friend and Brother Mahadeo,

I did not deserve your letter. I know how little I am able to do for India, although I may be willing; and if I am not even willing, it is my daily prayer, "God make me willing to do Thy will and to suffer in the fight for victory over evil".

130. As associate of Gandhi and former inmate in Gandhi's *ashram*.

Last week was very hard to pull through. I felt a little of all, what it meant for *Bapu*. He must have suffered more than we can think or say. Only this also: but faith in God and his righteous cause could give him strength to come through as the victorious. And once more has He proved to the world that spirit is the only thing which matters in this world, that truth will stand for ever, and that love is strong as ... and many waters cannot quench love.

I cannot help to believe that everywhere where the true fight for truth, goodness and righteousness is carried out with the greatest zeal then too will evil powers do their very best to destroy the good which is going on in the same place.

How wonderful great *Bapu* is; always looking away from himself and only desiring the good of others.

But how could he fast three days again? He must have got a complete victory over his whole body and mind but first when I heard he was alright after the fast I felt I was able to go about doing my daily duties again with a little bit of my old joy over life itself. But this time what St. Paul once said: "When one member suffereth, all the members suffers with it".

How good of you to send me that telegram!

I feel as if I cannot yet write to *Bapu*. His life, thoughts and sufferings are at the present time too sacred to be disturbed by anyone. But I am longing very much to write a letter to him and tell him many things.

You can know how thankful I was to have his letter from the two days arrest, but that day was nearly unbearable; and then to be so far away from all of you. You are there in the time of need and sorrow as well as the time of joy.

Give my love to *Bapu*, to all the *ashram* and to yourself from

Esther *Bahen*

P.S. If *Bapu* likes some more shirts made, I shall only be too glad to make them, you know, if you will send the material please. I've had a hard time spending the last week with my *real* friend among the Danes here, a lady doctor who now is going home to Denmark. She got consumption. She did her very best in trying to understand me whatever I ... did. Now she has gone. I am still more lonely amongst my own people the Danes.

Dear brother you ask for my blessing. I know only one blessing I love more than all others.

"The Lord bless thee and keep thee;
The Lord make his face shine upon thee,
And be gracious unto thee
The Lord lift his countenance upon thee,
And give thee peace".

Miss Faering to Gandhi, April 29, 1919[131]

My dear *Bapu*,

When I write again because something has been in my mind for a long time, I cannot help saying as an explanation for my writing that I know you need nobody to defend or praise you, and many persons can do that far better than I can, but it is partly for my own sake I have written this; for the sake of my peace of mind. And now I come and ask you *Bapu*, if you will not allow me to publish it in "*The Hindu*"[132] and other papers. I might easily have written much more and used much stronger expressions, but I know you do not like that. Is it too much to say that the principles of the State is not resting upon truth as its fundamental law?

131. SN6571.
132. A daily newspaper published in Madras.

I've today got permit to go to Kotagiri[133] for one month. I had to wait for them weeks for the reply. But what is the use of going to the hills when my mind and heart is far away in north India in *Satyagrahashram*,[134] when the fight for truth is going on?

How is your health *Bapu*!

With much love from your thankful child
Esther

April 29, 1919

A TRUTH-WITNESS

Long enough have I kept silence, because I am a Dane–a foreigner in India–have no right to take part or be interested in the affairs of India regarding political or important social matters. As a Dane, I have no right to speak as I feel, or act according to my conscience.

At least if I do so, my fate is sure–The Government will send me out of India. Although I am less a foreigner to India than many of the English people, who claim India to be theirs and behave in India as if they have the only right. I shall not speak about their right here, but I know only one right to India–the right gained by love and service.

I am only a very bad beginner trying to gain this right through love and sacrifice.

And so as a lover of India and her people will I speak humbly and quietly, and yet so loud that it may be heard too by those who do not like to hear it.

And shall it even cost me my privilege to stay in India I must speak, cannot keep silent; and shall I therefore leave, it will be with the greatest pain and with a bleeding heart. Yet I will rather leave India than stay if it is a crime to love her and take interest in the great problems of today.

133. The Danish Mission used this hill station for summer vacations.
134. The name of Gandhi's *ashram* on the banks of the Sabarmati River. It is now called "*Harijan Ashram*".

Then I can say with Tennyson: "It is better to have loved and lost than never to have loved at all". And yet I have not lost my love for India even if I shall leave her beautiful plains. No, the ties of love and affection will only grow stronger by the enforced separation.

I have called my article "A Truth-Witness".

Who is a truth-witness? Down through the ages there has been many a truth-witness, but the greatest, noblest truth-witness of our time is M.K. Gandhi, the Saint of today, Gandhi, the Truth-Witness.

Many Christians will maybe feel hurt in their minds when I dare to call Gandhi a Saint. I shall explain what I understand by the word a Saint. A Saint is one who his whole life makes it easier for people to believe in the loving God.

This implies a complete surrender of one's own will and a daily sacrifice of one's own self.

But Gandhi has in His life again and again shown clearly that He in this life, has accepted the highest law, the law of love; and so it is not too much to say that His whole being is love, love to all, a love which is able and willing to suffer for those who are ill-treated, despised and looked down upon by the world.

And so I call Gandhi a Saint. And here I confess as a Christian that never have I found the true mind of Christ copied so beautifully in the life of any Christian missionary as I found it in Gandhi's life. And when I speak about Christ's mind, there are two or three outstanding features which I make essential for the Christian life or character, namely: love, humility and truth.

Gandhi possesses all these qualities in the highest sense. Read about His life in South Africa, and you will find it to be true.

Many amongst us Christian missionaries have pride instead of humility and our passion for truth is not always directed in the right way, and our love for the people is more often felt as a kind of pity.

And so I frankly confess that the day I first met Mahatma Gandhi was a day of the greatest and sincerest humiliation for me as a Christian, but it became later the day of the richest blessing and joy and great help and inspiration.

Secondly I have called Gandhi a truth-witness. And so He is. He has only one passion, and that is the passion for truth; and for its sake has He suffered much, ... is still suffering much and will have to suffer as long as He lives.

But to suffer for the sake of truth is the noblest kind of suffering we can call down upon ourselves.

In this world is truth not esteemed by men rather despised, hated and overlooked by the world. And so when a truth-witness sounds the battle-cry for the sake of truth many will say: this mad fellow ought to be shut up in a cloister or prison or taken to some desolate island, where he is made harmless for the security of the State.

In their ignorance men will say so, not knowing that truth cannot be kept down by *bolt* or *bar*.

And throughout the world and ages, there have been men and women, who have suffered, gone to prison and death gladly, willingly and victoriously for the sake of truth.

So it may be right to say, when we live in a society where truth is *not* the fundamental law, "The right place for a just man is the prison". (Thoreau)

And so Mahatma Gandhi will live and suffer for the sake of truth, ye even die for the sake of truth and maybe first then His people to whom He gave all without keeping anything back for Himself will understand what real life is and then they will realise that the only way in which they can honour the memory of Mahatma Gandhi is by following love and truth as He did, then will all the sufferings not have been in vain.

When I wrote this I am very well aware of the result which can follow!

Therefore I want to underline that I write this as an individual; and the "Danish Mission Society" which sent me out does not agree with me and cannot at all understand these my views and opinions as far as they know them or have been told about it from other sides.

My fellow missionaries here in India, the Danes, will not understand me in this. They blame me, criticise me, misunderstand me, or pity me because "I have lost my true mission out of sight and gone astray". So I stand quite alone and neither the Danish Mission Society nor my fellow missionaries can be kept responsible or blamed for my position here in India. I am the only one who is responsible for what I feel, think and say, and I am quite willing to take the consequences of my actions.

Esther Faering
Danish missionary
Tirukoilur, S. Arcot
April 29, 1919

Miss Faering to Mahadev Desai, May 4, 1919[135]

"Bethany"
Kotagiri
May 4, 1919

My dear Brother Mahadeo,

The very same day I got your letter (27), I started to write again to you, but different kind of work and spiritual tiredness prevented me to stop.

Then the first of May I went to Kotagiri where I will stay for one month while my school is closed. But what is the use of going to the hills, when my mind is far away and my heart and thoughts are in the *ashram*. So nothing can help me here. Nature is wonderful here in all her majesty and abundance of beauty and charm, peace is prevailing in her calmness and quietness, but in the same country is these people who suffer and struggle, starve, fight for their existence and my friends suffer too and fight for truth and their human rights. How can I then be glad?

135. SN 6585.

You are right, it is too hard to be so far away from all of you; and very few here can understand me, and some will tease and mock me, which I don't care about, but rather take as a great honour.

All people say, I am so much changed during the last one or two months. I am looking 10 years older and have lost my natural joy. But is that strange? No, woe unto me, if I was the same today, as I was a month ago.

How are you yourself? I do remember how very kind you looked the day I left Madras but when we have learnt to take day by day, we shall get sufficient strength for the need(?) of each day. How is *Bapu's* health? As far as possible I follow your movements from the papers, but I should be very glad to get all *Bapu's* pamphlets and everything from his hand connected (from) with the *Satyagraha* movement. I have collected all the *Hindus* (papers) concerning this matter, and I want to go through them here on the hills.

The C.I.D.[136] has inquired in Tirukoilur if I had anything to do with the Sg,[137] and if I was the one who brought those school-girls in Villupuram St.[138] For me they can do as they like, only as I said often before, I should rather stay several years in prison than leave India; I do not know how I should live outside India without having my heart completely here.

It is difficult to give thanks always and for everything, but that is the only way through.

And I am only a very bad beginner in learning and practising in my life the lesson of true *satyagraha*.

With love to you and all in the *ashram*,

From yours affectionately

Esther *Bahen*

136. Central Intelligence Department.
137. *Satyagraha*?
138. Station.

Miss Faering to Gandhi, May 22, 1919[139]

"Faith Villa"
Kotagiri
May 22, 1919

My dear *Bapu*!

Can I take the *Swadesi*-vow? And how much does it mean? Does it mean, that I can never buy or receive anything from Denmark or let us say England, and does it include, that I ought not to keep and use, what I already have got in my house, partly from Denmark, and does it include everything, furniture and eatables as well as clothes and all other kind of articles?

When I have read in the *Hindu* for the last weeks about your plea for the *Swadesi*-vow, it has often been in my mind, that I should like to take this vow, only I should like to know the exact obligations which will follow, when I take it.

Mahadev wrote and told me that I now can send my application for my act of naturalisation. I am most willing and ready to do so. Only I wonder very much if the government under the present situation will bestow this favour or privilege upon me, whom they already have found out as a somewhat suspicious person. Anyhow, when I go down to Tirukoilur via Madras the 2nd of June, I shall see the Commissioner of Police, Mr. Armitage and make the requested oath before him.

I do feel, I am so very far away from the place, where the spiritual struggle and suffering for our sake is going on, and sometimes I wish I was free to go, wherever I want, instead of having to stay here on India's beautiful, glorious hills, being able to drink and take in all this perfect beauty, harmony and peace, which we can find everywhere in God's great, unlimited temple, when I can find and realise Him in a special way; and I can there trace His love and can even in the tiniest flower and grass, as well as I can admire His wonderful works, when I look upon the great solemn rock stretching its top towards heaven as in a sort of prayer

139. SN6620.

or unfilled longing and desire. But I ask myself again and again: "Why is it given you (me) to enjoy all this while millions of your (my) brothers and sisters down upon the hot plains suffer and starve, are sick and naked, without care and love, without work or at least joy in work, and so full of many kinds of care or anxiety?" What can I do? I have no excuse; and I feel more than ever before how poor and limited my love is, and how very few I can reach, because I am selfish and so far from that love, which is love of God, and therefore is ready to give up all, what belongs to self.

Bapu! When I stayed in Denmark, I did not realise how selfish, how proud, how narrow in my love, how little I care for truth, how little I know of the *whole* truth, how little I can suffer and bear and how I am fallen short of the ideal in every way; yes! I did not know myself, as I do now. But now I have only one desire, to make up for the past. I may forget and yet not forget the past, and then today and every day live, not for my own self but for all those who have claim upon me. I remember, you wrote once to me: "You have chosen the privilege of letting me be your brother; having made the choice, you must be content to suffer". So you wrote *Bapu*, two years ago; and now the time has come, when I every day feel it most painful that I am *not* able to suffer in a more actual way together with you. I may not be worthy of that just now, but I can pray that God, the Father, who is able and willing to give far above our poor requests, will give you all peace, all strength, all joy, all-conquering faith and final victory over all evil and darkness.

I am longing very much to hear from yourself, that you are well in spite of the overwhelming work, the problems, the sufferings for others sake and all the rest, which rests upon you unseen by most of us, and yet we do understand a little of the greatness of the task, which God again has given you, and the more we understand, the more can we pray in the right way, that the goal may be for the benefit and blessing and for the union of India and all her people.

With much love from yours thankful child

Esther

Please give my love to Mr. C. F. Andrews, if he is with you: I am very glad to know that he is with you.

V. Sundaram is lying ill in Coimbatore, he wrote, he was near death (cholera), he is now better: I hope to see him, when I go down to the plains.

I hope too that Mahadev is all right again.

Gandhi to Miss Faering, May 28, 1919[140]

Bombay, Wednesday [May 28, 1919]

My dear child,

Mahadev has made himself ill by his self-will. A self-willed friend, brother, son or secretary often fails at the critical moment. Mahadev is all these four rolled into one. At first I thought I would revenge myself upon him by fasting. In that case you would have come down upon me with that remarkable text from the Bible "Vengeance is mine". I am therefore adopting a less drastic method-doing the letter writing myself. It is a pleasurable sensation for me to do continuous writing for any length of time. My hand too works fairly steadily.

I wish you would not torture yourself so for not sharing the sorrows of those you love. For you to finish your agreement[141] is severe enough self-restraint. It is absolutely necessary. If you have real love, as I know you have, it must silently but more than less surely affect your present surroundings. In thought no act is lost, says the *Bhagavad Gita*. You are therefore doing your duty to the full by patiently and conscientiously doing your present work. Even the fresh energy you will get on the hills is to be used for the sake of your work. Why then worry?

The *swadeshi* vow extends to personal clothing only. I dare not ask you to deny yourself the use of Danish gifts from loved ones. It is enough if in future you buy only *swadeshi* cloth and let

140. *The Diary of Mahadev Desai*; *Collected Works*, Volume 15, page 331.

141. With the Danish Missionary Society.

your other things also be *swadeshi* so far as possible. We shall discuss greater changes when we meet again.

Mr. Andrews passed a few days with me. He is now in Delhi. Do tell Sundaram I was pained to hear of his illness. He must make himself healthy and strong.

With love,

Yours,
Bapu

Miss Faering to Gandhi, June 10, 1919[142]

Tirukoilur
June 10, 1919

My dear *Bapu* and *Guru*[143],

Again in Tirukoilur in the midst of all my children I must try to answer your letter which I got just before I left the hills. It is always a joyous event when the postman brings a letter from your hand, and so this time too I read it often, so I might get all you had to give me.

I shall try not to worry. It is in one sense a sin to worry because it shows I have no faith in God's care and love for those whom I love although I know He is both willing to keep them and protect them far better than I can.

It was a great joy for me to stop in Coimbatore and stay in Sundaram's home; he has got such a very dear mother.

We went the next day out to his village and he is then doing a great deal for his villagers. I liked very much to see their weaving-places--they make them real *swadesi*-work and they have got some splendid small handlooms for making a kind of very rough, coarse blankets. Sundaram promised to get me such a small handloom

142. SN6641.
143. teacher.

and put it up somewhere in my house and then I shall try to learn to weave. He has then a very great work before him. I only wish he might become stronger. He was rather weak and took very little or no food at all.

Then in Madras I went and saw Devadas. It is like something of "home" to see him, it was to me a great joy to find him keeping good health and faithfully doing his work, although he is going for the great task you have given him. But he has faith in his work and that means all. He gave me the first Hindi Reader and I wonder if I shall find him to learn Hindi when I somehow have mastered Tamil. When I came down from the hills, I got the very same day 200 girls back from the villages, and 100 new girls, nearly naked or in rags and very dirty and miserably thin. I love to see the change in their little faces and altogether when they are clean and combed. I am always happy when I stay with those children. They are like sunshine and then they are so innocent and unconscious. But I feel the responsibility of having so many girls to bring up and take care of, but they have come simply because it is famine time and so many starve and suffer, so we can't refuse them although we have no proper place at all. And I wish I could give them weaving work but it will take some time before I can do so.

Bapu, you do not know how very careless I am with my things. I have lost ever so many things since I came to India, simply because I am thoughtless or careless. I have lost my watch, waterproof, silver buttons, often money and so on. But this time when I came from Madras, I had just taken about 460 rupees from the bank for the school ... expenses. I kept them together with many things in a big handbag. When I changed in Villupuram, I had to go from one compartment to another. And first when I came home in Tirukoilur, I missed (all) the bag and all the money. I tell this to ask for your advice. Not for one moment I remembered this bag before it was too late. Now I think it is a very well deserved punishment because I often have been so careless. And I think that I, and nobody else, ought to suffer for my carelessness. So I have taken a loan in our church fund and will pay it back month by month. My father would send me the money if I asked him for it, but that wouldn't be fair. And I fear too the hard judgment he would pass upon me. I shall try to put my expenses down and live as simple as possible. That is not bad, rather good; and I need it. I take rice twice a day, but I take still coffee for my "*apam*"[144] in the morning. I find it difficult to give coffee up, and I have still got some coffee-beans in my house, but I ought to leave it off, when they are finished. There is only one difficulty: for one year I can't spend my money as I like to do. That I will find hard.

I don't feel the least sorry for the lost property and money, only am I very ashamed because of my carelessness. The punishment is well deserved, but I am not sure of the lesson which is most important to learn: to be careful for the future, or to keep less and less private property which you will miss when you lose them?

They have yet never sent me clothes out from Denmark. I have asked them only to send books, as I love my own Danish mother-tongue, and now and then enjoy to read it. It is a little difficult to get altogether *swadesi*-goods, it is so very easy with regard to the food question, but the cloth is more difficult to get, at least in Tirukoilur. And if I have understood rightly, it is the best way of exercising the *swadesi* by getting one's supply from the very place where we live. Sundaram promised to supply me with all what I need from Coimbatore but it is rather far away.

V. S. Venkataraman advised me to go to the local magistrate in Tirukoilur for the sake of the oath,[145] which must be said before a magistrate and then send the memorial-act to the Governor. I will do so one of the very first days, but as we have got so many new girls and six new, quite young teachers, I found no time just in the first week. I love to be down at the plains again, although it is very hot and dry here. I do hope that Mahadeo is quite well again and fit for work again, so he can help you in all the heavy work, which largely depends upon you. I fear, I too am very self-

144. a breakfast dish like pancake.
145. For naturalisation.

willed, all say at least so. I try to follow the affairs and important matters in "*The Hindu*" and I am surprised when I read about the martial law in Punjab, and it is a shame to be from Europe.

If Sundaram not yet has written I promised to give his deep love and thanks for the message from you when I wrote.

Devadas sang for us the beautiful national hymn he sang the 6th of April.[146]

Allow me to send this proof from our weaving department. I only fear I have cut it too little.

With much love from your thankful child

Esther

How is "*Ba*"[147] in the *ashram* with all her new five children? I did like to read Tagore's letter to the Viceroy[148] and Mr. Andrews too is not afraid to say his opinion. India is undergoing a process of purification and she will become more unified, purified and gain her natural birthright, when she is safe through the trial.

I read Tolstoy's life and teaching at the present time. Tolstoy has for many years been the one who gave me much to think

146. April 6, 1919 was observed as a day of nation-wide protest against repressive legislation.
147. *Ba*–mother. Gandhi's wife, Kasturba, was addressed by the inmates of the *ashram* as "*Ba*".
148. Rabindranath Tagore, who was awarded the Nobel Prize for literature in 1913, wrote to the Viceroy of India on May 30, 1919, giving up his knighthood in protest against the massacre of demonstrators in Jallianwala Bagh and the insults and sufferings imposed on the people of the Punjab. "The time has come", he wrote, " when badges of honour make our shame glaring in the incongruous context of humiliation, and I for my part, wish to stand, shorn of all special distinctions, by the side of those of my countrymen who, for their so called insignificance, are liable to suffer degradation not fit for human beings".

about and who never lets one be satisfied with anything half or below the ideal.

Miss Faering to Gandhi, June 20, 1919[149]

June 20, 1919

My dear *Bapu*!

I do hesitate, before I write this letter, but at the same time I can't help to tell you this. I know you will understand me and forgive me that I add my care to all the care you already have. Two days ago the Police Inspector came to my house, and he told me he had special order from Madras Government to follow my movements. I had to answer so many questions, but I regard only the two following as somewhat important.

(1) Where will you go, if you have to leave India?

I answered, I do not at all intend to leave India with my good will at least.

(2) What is your pursuit by staying in India? (Tirukoilur)

I answered, "I desire to serve my school girls by teaching them to become good *Indian* women, who know and love their own country, its customs and language; besides that, I desire to live as a Christian in their midst more than merely to preach Christianity".

This has now been sent to the Madras Government; and I do not know, what the result will be, but I know Mr. Bittmann has been called to see the Governor's Secretary on behalf of me.

If I say, I have no fear, I am not true. I do fear they will send me out of India, and that will be the hardest blow and punishment for me. I do wonder whether censor opens my letters to you *Bapu*.

I wish I could go and see you and talk with you.

149. SN6668.

On the 22nd, the 30th birthday of mine, I have decided to take the *swadesi*-vow, but I will have to use, what I still have got of Danish or English goods because I lost those moneys, I am in one way very glad I lost them; I think I needed it.

I send my love and reverence.

Your child Esther

I hope Mahadeo[150] is keeping good health again.

Miss Faering to Gandhi, June 25 and 30, 1919[151]

June 25,1919

My very dear *Bapu* and *Guru*!

It may be the very last letter I am permitted to send you but no government upon earth can prevent me from looking upon you as my spiritual Father, *Guru* and ideal of life; and nobody can prevent me from getting help and inspiration from you. When I look upon you, I realise, that some reach only through sufferings to true joy and peace. And we get the perfect victory only when we have conquered our own selves.

I value life and things in quite a new way since I met you and the day must come where I am willing and ready to live as one who depends only upon God, fearless of men and their judgment. I have much to learn, much to give up and abandon from my life as a hindrance for my perfection and fulfilment of God's purpose with me here in life. But when I feel weak, your example shall inspire me.

June 30

My very dear *Bapu*!

150. Mahadev Haribhai Desai, secretary to Gandhi.
151. SN6680.

Today I received your precious letter,[152] and I must write at once.

Mr. Bittmann came last week and had a talk with me about all this matter.

He said I had the choice between my work and what he called "my taking part or interest in Indian politic". He said I was not called upon to take the least part in Indian politic, firstly because as I came out as a missionary, secondly because I was a Dane and not only a guest in India but in *British* India. That I am a guest in India I always remember, although I feel at home here.and always have been treated not so much as a guest but more as a member of the home and family, but I may have overlooked that I am a guest in British India too.

I told Mr. Bittmann that I was very willing to resign and leave the Danish mission if my behaviour might cause any or even the least harm to the mission as a whole body. I was without the least fear for my own person, as I feel in the same way as you wrote: whatever happens will be for the best or my best. But I did not like to think that I in a way was responsible for the welfare of all the Danish missionaries in India, then rather before it was too late stand alone apart from the D.M.S.

But if I left D.M.S., I might probably ... have to leave India, as I fear I should not be allowed to go to the place where I love to stay–and what then.

Mr. B. said I had only one thing to do at the present, to keep perfectly quiet and leave off all correspondence with all who in any way are connected with any political work. I really never intended to take or play any part in Indian politic. That task ... for more experienced and competent people than I am or ever shall be. But I should never deny that all my sympathy is with the people of India, her joys are mine too, her sorrows are mine. She has given me so much, so how can I show ungrateful to her. And to say that I have to give up every visible contact with you *Bapu* or Mr. C.F. Andrews is more than to starve me. I would call it a small thing if they took all my property; I might even feel more

152. Please see next item.

free and happy. But to fetter my soul with different kind of restrictions, is unworthy for me to accept, and I would feel as Judas, the traitor if I promised never to write to you as long as you allow me to call you by the sacred name "*Bapu*" and regard me as your child Esther although I am not worthy of that name, but I try to become more and more worthy of it.

Dear *Bapu*, I might very well act in haste but in this case I had not the feeling of anger. I felt only very, very sad by the very thought that I maybe would have to leave India after such a short but happy stay where I have been receiving good from India in so many ways.

I can understand that I might not take any public part in India's politic, and I have promised Mr. Bittmann not to have anything to do with politic in one or another way. If I have, he will simply have to send me home to Denmark and excommunicate me from the Danish Mission Society, because they did not send me out for any political purpose.

On the other hand they have nobody else at the present to do my work. We have now more than 200 girls, and I love to stay amongst them. So they say it is my first duty to look after the work God ... has given me and for its sake sacrifice all other interests which may hinder me in doing my work. Surely, if I had only to give up some sorts of interests as playing tennis or reading books, I should give it up with the greatest joy but here is something much more than interests.

I will of course follow your advice and keep quiet until I receive any further order or instructions.

I may not be able to write but my thoughts will daily follow you in the task which claims all your faith, strength, courage and sacrifice. And I will pray to God–that He Himself, the God of all life, of all peace, of all hope may be with you in all your ways. He only knows our hearts. It has always been a comfort to me, that He knows us through and through, our motives and aspirations. Thus it matters so very little if there are sides of our being which no one but God seems to be able to apprehend.

About tomorrow or about the future, I know nothing.

I only know we cannot drift beyond His love and care. So I am cheerfully ... day by day.

With much love from yours for ever thankful child Esther

I find it in one way very humiliating that my letters to you and other persons have been opened. What I called a Truth-Witness has been opened.

As far as I know Mr. Bittmann, he wants to be indifferent or as an outsider in my affair only because he is our Chairman. He has to move in this matter.

I am only thankful because you, *Bapu*, in the midst of all your work would plead for me too, but I will write again when I know more than today.

I shall try to get spinning wheels as well as handlooms for my girls.

Gandhi to Miss Faering, June 27, 1919[153]

Laburnum Road,
Bombay,
June 27, 1919

My dear child,

Your letter just received makes me extremely sad. I cannot conceive the possibility of their deporting you.[154] But if they should, you have to cheerfully submit to the fate. If you wish me to, I shall gladly correspond with the Government. I may fail in my attempt. That would not matter. My advice to you also is that if they impose conditions on which alone you could stay, you should accept the conditions in so far as they are not humiliating.

153. *My Dear Child*, pages 36-37; *Collected Works*, Volume 15, pages 393-94.

154. Miss Faering apparently felt that the government intended to deport her from India because of her friendship with Gandhi.

I may commence in my person civil disobedience next week. It is therefore at the present moment hardly possible for us to meet.

As for *swadeshi*, there is no need for you to discard what you have from home. It is enough for you to confine all your present need to *swadeshi* things. The vow is only restricted to personal clothing.

Subject to your Board's[155] consent, you should introduce spinning-wheels in your school.

Regarding yourself, I suggest also your consulting Mr. Bittmann and being guided by him. Shall I write to him? I am so anxious that not a single step be taken by you in haste or in anger. Then whatsoever happens will be for the best. Please write to me often.

With deep love,

Written in haste and unrevised.

Yours,
Bapu

[Gandhi wrote to Mr. Sundaram on August 17: "When are you going to Miss Faering?"[156] Mr. Sundaram visited her and reported to Gandhi that she had resigned from the DMS and was afraid of being deported.

Gandhi immediately wrote to Lord Willingdon, Governor of Bombay, through his private secretary, on August 22, appealing against the deportation of Miss Faering[157]:

"Probably the name of Miss Esther Faering, of Danish extraction and, up to recently, if not still, working as Superintendent of a Girls' School belonging to the mission in Tirukoilur, has been brought to His Excellency's notice. It was probably two years ago that she, along with another Danish lady,

155. Of the Danish Missionary Society.
156. SN3199.
157. SN6823; *Collected Works*, Volume 16, pages 57-58.

visited my *ashram* at Ahmedabad. Both the ladies took a special fancy for the *ashram* and its ideals. Miss Faering has since then met me three or four times and she has visited the *ashram*, I believe, once after her first visit. She has been a fairly regular correspondent and I believe she is attached to me like a child to its father, simply because, in her opinion, I represent in action the ideals she would fain enforce in her own life and is ever trying to. She loves India as her own motherland and I know it would be a terrible wrench to her if she is ever banished from India, as she dreads she might. Latterly, it seems she has been a suspect, very much shadowed.

It was her intention some time ago to leave the Danish mission, if she could. I think I succeeded in weaning her from the desire. I told her that it was her duty to fulfill her contract with the mission, so long as she was permitted to do so. I have just heard that she is no longer in the mission. If this is true and if she is permitted, I would be pleased to take her into the *ashram* where she would be associated with me in my non-political work. I believe her to be as truthful and straight a person as is to be found anywhere. She ever lives in the fear of God and does her best to live a Christian life. As her desire is to pass her life mostly in the midst of the people of India, I advised her to become naturalised. I know she took steps in the direction and I revised for her the petition for naturalisation. But I do not know whether she has sent it. I can only hope that His Excellency will meet her and form the same opinion about her that I have. If any undertaking is required about her, it can be easily given. If an assurance is necessary, I wish to assure His Excellency that I have not the slightest desire to avail myself of her services in the political field.

As probably Lord Willingdon is aware, the largest part of my work is social and moral or religious. My most intimate associates take hardly any part in my political work. The inmates of the *ashram* are engaged in agricultural, industrial and educational work, and if Miss Faering comes to the *ashram*, she will take part in these activities, and if need be, I will undertake, in no other.

"Miss Faering knows nothing about this letter but I am sending her a copy for the consolation that I am not unmindful of my duty to her as a privileged friend, as also for her endorsement of the under-taking I am promising herein.

"I tender my apology for troubling His Excellency on a matter of a partly personal nature".

He also wrote to the Governor of Madras.[158]

On the same day, he wrote to C.F. Andrews:[159]

"I have most disquieting news about Miss Faering from Sundaram. I asked him specially to go and see her. He has been there and he tells me she is no longer in the Danish mission and that she is in distress lest she might have to leave India. It would be almost death to her if she is forced to do so. Here is a copy of my letter to Lord Willingdon. I feel most keenly about her. Will you not immediately go to Madras and do what you can to prevent her banishment?...

"I do want you to agree with me that it is just as important to do our best to protect Miss Faering from harm as it is for me to resist the Rowlatt Act with my life and for you to be at Santiniketan".

On August 22, 1919, Mr. Sundaram sent to Gandhi the following letter he had received from Miss Faering:[160]

"Dear Sundaram,

"Monday I received a letter from our Chairman, kind and sympathetic; containing 400 rupees to pay my debt; given to me as a gift from the mission; they do not want to make life more difficult for me than it already is, they want to remove this 'stone' from my path; moreover there will be no conference or discussion concerning me, as they all feel they cannot ask me to come back, however much they regret and feel sorry because I leave the D.M.S.[161]

158. C.B. Dalal, compiler, *Gandhi, 1915-1948; A Detailed Chronology.* The text of the letter is not available.
159. SN6822; *Collected Works*, Volume 16, pages 58-59.
160. SN6821.
161. Danish Missionary Society.

"I am on leave until we have the answer from Denmark and therefore not allowed to take up any other work, before the home board's answer will be here. They want me to go back to Denmark but I cannot do so. I belong to India today more than ever before; about that, Sundaram, I cannot tell you now today...

"I am thinking much about the spinning and weaving, I should love to do that work and I shall give you my definite answer as soon as possible.

"Give *Bapu* my love

Esther"

Gandhi to Miss Faering, August 24, 1919[162]

Laburnum Road,
Bombay,
August 24, 1919

My dear child,

Sundaram's letter about you had made me very gloomy. My heart goes out to you in your sorrow. But I know that if we trust in God when we are weakest, somehow He makes us strong. Deep down in me therefore there is the feeling that all would be well with you no matter what happens to you. I could not, however, restrain myself from writing to the Governor. Here is a copy of my letter to him. If you are free, you would come down at once to the *ashram*. I want to write to Mr. Bittmann but I shall await reply to this. You will know the rest from my letter to the Governor. If it does not represent the situation correctly in any way, you will please let me know. You will be an unworthy child if you will not let me know your pecuniary wants.

With love,

Yours,
Bapu

162. *My Dear Child*, page 37; *Collected Works*, Volume 16, page 59.

Miss Faering to Gandhi, August 25, 1919[163]

August 25, 1919

My very dear *Bapu*!

What shall I write and how? Words are too poor to tell you how thankful, how happy I shall be, if I am allowed to come to the *ashram*, my home, which I love more than any other place in the whole world. I feel I should like to start tomorrow for the *ashram*; I am longing to come there and learn how to serve better and how to love more. Yes, *Bapu*! I am an unworthy child of you, but I do love you, as a child loves and trusts its father, and like a child owes its father everything, so I owe everything to you, since I met you on the 6th of January 1917, that day will for ever be the best, the greatest day in my life. *Bapu*! How can I ever thank you, because you for my sake wrote to H.E. Lord Willingdon? I can only say, I am very, very happy God is always most good towards His most unworthy children, and I can trace His love throughout my life, even now in this time I have passed through days full of sorrow and anxiety. I have felt it in this time that when we are weak He will make us strong, and I told Sundaram to tell you *Bapu*, that I was *happy* in spite of sorrow and I felt often that your sympathy and love gave me all the joy and strength I needed. I never felt alone. Now I do not belong to the Danish Mission for many reasons; and they nearly all asked me to go home to Denmark, but I said, *no, no*, I have only one desire, one purpose to stay in India, if I may be permitted to do so and give the little I can give.

Bapu I was asked not to write to you, before I had the answer from our home-board, but now I cannot help it; I simply must write to you. In reality I do not belong to the Danish Mission from the very day I had to write and resign as a worker there. It was a very great joy to see Sundaram and have your message (from you) and hear about you. I wonder, *Bapu*, how you in spite of all your heavy work can find time to take care of my sorrows and my cares too, and yet I know why it is so; to you love is law and law is love,

163. SN6825.

so you can always feel for everyone even the least amongst all those you have taken into your sympathy and confidence. God help me never to disappoint you.

After Sundaram left me, I had a letter from Mr. Bittmann telling me that the Mission had paid my debt (those c. 500 Rs. I lost) because they did not like to add to what I already had of difficulties; but I care for nothing, nothing of what I call mine. I can leave it gladly, if I may come to the *ashram*; I am only longing to do some work again: Miss Petersen will take my work from the 2nd of September. I have disappointed her, but we never know what is best for us. I am quite well again, and have joy and peace.

Miss Petersen came back from Denmark just a week ago. It was of course a great shock for her to receive just as she came, but she is very sympathetic.

Only last Saturday the Police Inspector came to see me and advised me to go and see Lord Willingdon in person. But is it not rather strange, that there has been so much talking and so many rumours, and they were just about sending me home for the sake of the Mission, and then Mr. Bittmann himself went to see the Chief Secretary; but he did not know anything, but the Commissioner of Police and the C. I. D.[164] must in one way be quite a separate department. Anyhow our Chairman has been warned and given the advice not to keep me in the Danish Mission and many missionaries told me, I ought not to stay in the mission.

I had never any taste for politic itself, but I find it difficult or impossible to be indifferent in matters, were I have all my heart and sympathy, but I have no other or greater desire than to come and stay in the *ashram* as a member of the family, happy to be counted worthy to live in the midst of many who have only one aim and purpose-how they can serve and love India and make themselves fit for this sacred work and duty. As Miss Petersen quite unexpected has to step into my work without any experience at all of this school I promised her to stay for a short time, a fortnight or so, and help her in this new work. But when I have obtained Lord Willingdon's permission to come to the *ashram*, I

164. Criminal Investigation Department.

shall come as soon as possible, and come with a heart full of joy and thanks to you and to all my friends and little brothers and sisters in the *ashram*, because of your readiness to give me a home, where I can enjoy all the rights and privileges of a child and the responsibilities too. I shall write to my father at home in Denmark and tell him that instead of feeling sorry for my sake he must rejoice with me. It is only because he never has been in India that he finds it somehow difficult to understand me when I tell him all about India, and how one simply can't help to love India, when one has discovered her as a little child little by little discovers the great wonders of its surroundings and feels what it is to be. He should just come to India, I should soon make him to see with my eyes and love, what I love. He is not coming, but if he knows I am happy, he too will be happy, whether I am near or far away, whether I am in Denmark or India.

Hoping and trusting and looking forward to my going to the *ashram* I send my love and all my thanks

from yours ever thankful
child Esther

It pains me that Sundaram is so weak and very often suffering but he has learnt something of the joy in sufferings.

When I came down from the hills the Police Inspector told me that it was quite useless for me to try to become naturalised....

Gandhi to Miss Faering, after August 25, 1919[165]

[After August 25, 1919]

My dear child,

You have been writing fairly regularly but I have been unable to do so. You know the reason why.

165. *My Dear Child*, pages 38-39; *Collected Works*, Volume 16, pages 62-63.

The pain I suffered was really nothing. Chhotalal made more of it than was deserved. I am taking all reasonable care of the body.

I take it that there is no hurry about your giving a final answer to the Board or Mr. Bittmann. Yours is a difficult case. I am most anxious that you should be absolutely true and faithful to the Board and that they should not in any way feel that you had done anything unworthy. Shall I write to Mr. Bittmann (am I spelling his name correctly? I have not your letter by me) even as I wrote to the Governor? Your service to India should be rendered as a true Dane and a Christian. You are serving because your Christianity prompts you to do so. And it is not enough that you feel so, it is necessary that your people should realise it through your love, humility and nobility. I do not know how best it can be done. Anyway your letters to them should be gentle, true and charitable... never harsh, bitter or reproachful. After all, yours in a way is a rebellion and it can only be justified by success in the religious sense of the term, even as Daniel's and Bunyan's were justified.

I am glad you are keeping well. Are you comfortable? You will be a bad child if you fail to express your wants to me. If you are in need of money, you will not hesitate to tell me so.

It is a strange phenomenon-everybody wanting to learn English.[166] You should satisfy their desire within bounds. Do tell me a little more fully as to who wants it.

With love,

Yours,
Bapu

166. Miss Faering apparently wrote to him of the desire of parents at her school that their children should be taught English.

Miss Faering to Gandhi, September 15, 1919[167]

Kallakurichi
September 15, 1919

My dear *Bapu,*

Sundaram[168] wrote me a short letter yesterday telling me that the Governor has given me permission to go to the *ashram.*

I read it again and again, and it gave me new hope and joy, *Bapu*! I am sure, you will let me come. I am looking forward to come. When I got your letter to the Governor, I sent a copy to E.K. Menon[169] and he is both glad and thankful because I can stay in the *ashram,* until he can claim me–if he ever can.

He has only one aim–to serve India and his people. He is a true Indian, and now he is trying to become a true *Swadesi*[170].

Bapu, may I come soon; I can be ready to start for Sabarmati Monday the 22nd. I got a slight attack of influenza, when I came to Kallakurichi, but am alright again, so I can go to Tirukoilur Wednesday, settle everything with Miss Petersen and then leave for Madras Saturday night, stay with the Bittmanns Sunday and then Monday go to Sabarmati.

With love from your thankful child

Esther

167. SN6875.
168. V.A. Sundaram of Coimbatore in south India was an early inmate of Gandhi's *ashram.* He later became assistant to the founder of the Benares Hindu University, Pandit Madan Mohan Malaviya.
169. Miss Faering was engaged to Mr. Menon in February 1920.
170. "*Swadeshi*" ("*swadesi*") literally means "of one's own country". The *Swadeshi* movement–to buy Indian and boycott foreign goods, especially textiles from Britain–was a protest against British rule.

Miss Faering to Gandhi, September 21, 1919[171]

[In a letter dated September 15, Miss Faering expressed her longing to go to the *ashram* soon.]

Kallakurichi
S. Arcot
September 21, 1919

My dear *Bapu*!

Thank you! Thank you, because I may come. I am more thankful than I can tell you today.

Sundaram's information was not quite correct. Mr. C.F. Andrews' information was different. He told me that the Governor of Madras was willing to let me go to the *ashram*, and he would write to the Bombay Governor and place the matter before him. So I will have to be patient for some few days more, as Mr. Andrews asked me to stay quietly and not go to the *ashram*, before the final answer came. But every day is a trial for me, as long as I have no real work to do, so I shall be very much looking forward to your answer.

With love from your thankful child

Esther

P.S. Your wire gave me great comfort.

Miss Faering to Gandhi, September 27, 1919[172]

Kallakurichi
September 27, 1919

My dear *Bapu*!

How is it that it is your birthday both the 21st of September and the 2nd of October.

171. SN6891.
172. SN6900.

May be it is only to give people, who are too late to congratulate you on the 21st another chance on the 2nd of October. I am too late for the 21st, but I hope not for the 2nd birthday.

I have nothing to give; if we are in debt to somebody, we cannot give anything, but try to pay of the debt.

But I shall not attempt what is impossible; my heart is full of thanks to you *Bapu* for all what you have meant for me in the past year: and words seem too poor to express what we feel, and we can only wonder and feel how unworthy we are to receive God's best to man.

I mean *Bapu*, the gift, the privilege, that you will count me amongst your friends.

And when it again is your birthday I can only wish and pray for, that all your hopes and expectations for India and her people may be fulfilled; that all your sufferings, labour and efforts may be crowned with success, and bear the finest and most perfect fruit in the "Young India", those who are going to create the destinate of India's future.

And may your message of love and *satyagraha* sound all over India and find a response in the hearts of all those who love India with a pure heart. So a new spirit will regenerate India, the spirit which she has seen revealed in and through you *Bapu*!—the spirit of love, self-lessness, fearlessness and truth. Then we shall see our sacred India conquer the world—not by force or violence, but by truth and love. And other nations will come and ask for her blessings and take their seat at her sacred feet to learn the great, eternal truth about love's triumph over her enemy--(yea) even over death. May the year to come be rich in joy, even amidst struggle, work, tumult and sorrow.

With much love from your thankful child

Esther

Miss Faering to Gandhi, September 29, 1919[173]

Kallakurichi,
September 29, 1919

Dear *Bapu*,

Forgive me, that I am impatient and writing again about myself. I am not ungrateful for what you have done already, but I find it so very hard to live in this way without work for about two months and in one way a burden to others.

The Governor, of course, cannot understand that I am longing, longing to get a decision. It is of no interest for him, cannot be of any interest to him, but if it would be useful, I should gladly go to Bombay and see the Governor and ask for permission and tell him how much I want to go to the *ashram*, and that I shall take no part at all in politics. If I was tired and needed rest, I should be most thankful to stay for a while with my friends here but I need only work. I feel every day I do not deserve the daily bread I eat; people ask me so many questions; and I am getting mentally tired and I am losing courage; I know it is very wrong of me, if I have faith in God and His purpose with my life, but this strange feeling of uncertainty is a weakening sort of feeling.

Will you allow me to go to Bombay and see the Governor?

With love

Yours thankful child
Esther

173. SN6902.

Gandhi to Miss Faering (telegram), October 4, 1919[174]

[Ahmedabad,
October 4, 1919]

PLEASE HAVE PATIENCE, HAVE MYSELF TELEGRAPHED GOVERNOR MADRAS EXPEDITE YOUR COMING.

[On October 4, Gandhi sent a telegram to the Governor of Madras in which he said[175]:

"MR. ANDREWS WROTE SAYING HIS EXCELLENCY WOULD EXPEDITE MISS FAERING'S COMING TO ME. SHE IS NOW WITHOUT OCCUPATION AND MOST ANXIOUS JOIN ME. WILL HIS EXCELLENCY PLEASE PERMIT MISS FAERING TO JOIN ME PENDING ANY INVESTIGATIONS HIS EXCELLENCY MIGHT BE MAKING".

The Private Secretary to the Governor, Mr. Droff, replied[176]: "... if Miss Faering will apply in the usual way to Government for permission to travel to Bombay, there will be no difficulty in granting it". Gandhi acknowledged this letter on October 22 and wrote to Mr. Droff[177]: "Will you please convey to His Excellency my thanks for the consideration shown about Miss Esther Faering who has now arrived at the *Satyagraha Ashram*".]

174. SN6932; *Collected Works*, Volume 16, page 208.
175. SN6931; *Collected Works*, Volume 16, page 208.
176. *Collected Works*, Volume 16, page 208.
177. *Ibid.*, p. 251.

Miss Faering to Gandhi, October 10, 1919[178]

Kallakurichi
October 10, 1919

My dear *Bapu*,

I was happy when I got your letter, although I feel ashamed over my impatience; and I did not deserve any letter from you, I know how much work is resting upon you. But, when Sundaram now nearly one month ago wrote to me "Lord W. has been pleased to allow you to go to the *ashram*, and you can go within some few days", I was very happy. And when I then got to know that I still had to wait, it was a very bitter disappointment for me, nearly too much, after I had been so happy by the very thought that I could go to the *ashram*.

I did not know, that (vest) was made of foreign yarn; if I had only known, of course I would never have sent you that. It was my fault, I did not know better, and I can only see one way in which I can make my fault good again, firstly by trying to learn to weave, and then make you another one; secondly, I will ask them to get Indian yarn in our industrial schools and *not* foreign yarn. We-or they, ought I to say-are getting the spinning wheels both in Tiruvannamalai and Tirukoilur.

I told Mrs. Bjerrum not to write, but she did so[179] and I feel ashamed of that too, because it shows I am very selfish and cannot forget myself; but when I got your wire last Saturday, I got all the help I needed. I came to myself, and I repeat many times a day the

178. SN6939.
179. Mrs. Emilie Bjerrum, a Danish missionary then in Kallakurichi, wrote to Gandhi on October 2, 1919:
"... You perhaps know that our dear little sister Esther Faering is staying with us. We have been so very glad to have her company and we shall indeed be sorry to part with her again, but in spite of that we cannot help seeing how she is suffering in mind because she is without work and because she is longing so much to go to *ashram* where she will be able to live and work for her beloved India.
"She is longing to go there, and is longing to see you and is longing for physical work. Every day when the postman disappoints her

words "have patience" and although I am longing as intensely as ever before for the permission to go to the *ashram*. I try at the least now to make the best out of my time here and do not allow my thoughts to wander idly here and there.

But if there is no answer during the next week, I should like with your permission to go to Madras and see the Governor, who will return Wednesday next from his tour.

Yes *Bapu*, when I had no letter from you for a long while, I feared, I had lost something undiscovered but very precious to me, and I felt unhappy. Now I am happy again.

With love from your thankful child

Esther

Gandhi to Miss Faering, October 23, 1919[180]

On the train,
Thursday [October 23, 1919][181]

My dear child,

I do want you to feel at home at the *ashram*. I do not want you to feel or think you are in the midst of strangers. Pick up a few words in Hindustani daily and the linguistic barrier will vanish.

she gets so downhearted and she sometimes thinks that God has forsaken her and does not want her service.

"When you wrote to her that you had written to Lord Willingdon on her behalf she became very happy and took it as a token from God that He still had a work for her in India.

"But she is not so strong as she might be. All the cares and anxiety have worked upon her nerves and therefore it is hard for her to wait quietly for the answer. We love to have her with us but we want to see her happy. If you would write her a word of cheer I am sure it would be of such(?) help to her. She loves and admires you more than anybody else.

"This is the reason why I have bothered you with my letter--forgive me please... (SN6919)

180. *My Dear Child*, page 41; *Collected Works*, Volume 16, page 253.

181. Gandhi left on a tour of the Punjab soon after Miss Faering arrived at the *ashram*.

If the *ashram* is your home, you must reproduce the necessary home comfort. Pray demand them. Send me a line daily.

Remember that love is never afraid, it has *no secrets*. You will therefore open your heart to all and you will, I doubt not, find a response in every heart. Love will not be denied for it is ever patient and ever suffering. And love is service, therefore it ever rejoices in service.

Do keep your health.

Yours sincerely,
M. K. Gandhi

[On October 23, Gandhi wrote to his nephew, Maganlal, who was managing the *ashram*, to "make what arrangements you think best for Miss Faering", and added: "If you take her out for a walk every morning, as I used to take you out, this flower will bloom the better and will give sweet fragrance".[182]]

Gandhi to Miss Faering, October 24, 1919[183]

c/o Sarladevi Choudhrani,
Lahore,
October 24, 1919

My dear child,

This is just to tell you you are with me in thought. I had a most wonderful experience here.[184]

With love,

Yours
Bapu

182. *Collected Works*, Volume 16, page 254.
183. *My Dear Child*, page 44; *Collected Works*, Volume 16, page 254.
184. The reference apparently is to the reception accorded to Gandhi on arrival at Lahore.

Gandhi to Miss Faering, [October 27,] 1919[185]

Lahore,
Monday [October 27,] 1919

My dear child,

I have your letter.

I am having a precious time here. I may not be able to come [to the *ashram*] in the early part of November after all.

Mr. Andrews is here and we often talk of you.

Keep good health please.

With love,

Yours,
Bapu

Gandhi to Miss Faering, [October 28, 1919][186]

Lahore,
[October 28, 1919]

My dear child,

I have your two letters. I leave [for] Delhi today with Mr. Andrews.

I am glad you are feeling at home there. I am most anxious that you should retain your health and get stronger than you are. The best thing of course is not to worry about anything. Be careful for nothing and to take or prepare the diet that suits you.

Ba[187] wrote to me you were looking after her.

185. *My Dear Child*, page 43; *Collected Works*, Volume 16, page 263.
186. *My Dear Child*, pages 42-43; *Collected Works*, Volume 16, page 264.
187. Kasturba, wife of Gandhi. Inmates of *ashram* called her *Ba* or mother.

I may some time describe the work here.[188] It is difficult work but it is useful and people gain by it.

Please do not write for *Young India*[189] at present. I do not want to disturb the Government though there is nothing wrong about your writing on the educational system. For the time being let your life speak to your surroundings.

With love,
Bapu

Gandhi to Miss Faering, [October 31,] 1919[190]

Delhi,
Friday [October 31,] 1919

My dear child,

You will teach the children[191] not so much reading and writing as what is character and what it means. It therefore gives me much joy to know that you will soon be coming in close touch with the children.

Please tell Sundaram to write to me as also Krishna and Manidatta.

I am not likely to return yet for a fortnight.

Mr. Andrews is with me and we are both trying to bring about peace.

I wonder if the coming of the children causes some over-crowding and inconvenience.

Yours,
Bapu

188. Gandhi was then collecting evidence on repression and atrocities committed by the authorities in the Punjab province to suppress the freedom movement.
189. Weekly newspaper of Gandhi.
190. *My Dear Child*, pages 41-42; *Collected Works*, Volume 16, pages 268-69.
191. Children in the *ashram*.

Gandhi to Miss Faering, [after November 4, 1919][192]

Lahore,
[After November 4, 1919]

My dear child,

I have your sweet letters. But you will not expect regular replies from me for the time being. I am having rich experiences of life. When you render yourself a willing instrument of service, inexpressible joy is the reward. But more later or when we meet.

With love,

Yours,
Bapu

Gandhi to Miss Faering, December 4, 1919[193]

Lahore,
December 4, 1919

My dear child,

Why have you become ill? You ought not to take upon yourself tasks which are beyond you. You are not capable of going 3rd class to Bombay. Indeed you need not have gone to Bombay. However do be well quickly by asking for all the service you may need. What was the matter with you? Mr. Mahadev has described your malady somewhat. Please tell me all about it.

With love and prayers,

Yours,
Bapu

192. *My Dear Child*, page 43; *Collected Works*, Volume 16, page 287.
193. *My Dear Child*, page 24; *Collected Works*, Volume 16, page 328.

Gandhi to Miss Faering, [December 7] 1919[194]

Lahore,
[December 7,] 1919

My dear child,

I have your two letters including the long one. You have done well in sending it. As I have already said, you have come to the *ashram* not to lose your Christianity, but to perfect it.

If you don't feel the presence of God at the prayer meetings, then remember that the names Rama and Krishna signify the same as Jesus to you.

You should most decidedly not attend these meetings and you should pray in your private chamber. The prayer meetings are not meant to force anyone into a position. They are meant for free men and women. The children must attend. Those who abstain from sheer laziness must attend. But for you, no one can misunderstand your abstinence. You will therefore please do that which gives you the greatest peace. The *ashram* is nothing if it does not enable you to realise God more and more fully day by day. If on Sundays or any other days you would go to Church, of course you shall do so.

I am so glad you have given me that long and beautiful letter and enabled me to enter more fully into your heart. Your coming is a joy to me. It will be a greater joy, if upon experience you find it gives you peace, health and real joy and if it thereby enables the other Christians to see that God and Christianity can be found also in institutions that do not call themselves Christian and that truth is the same in all religions though through refraction it appears for the time being variegated even as light does through a prism.

I feel like you that it is too early for you to go to Madras even to meet Miss Petersen. Will she not come to the *ashram*? She ought to. Let her come and see it in its new habitation and feel its progress if there is any made. Please give her my love.

194. *My Dear Child*, pages 45-46; *Collected Works*, Volume 16, page 333.

I do hope you have now completely recovered. You should not trifle with your body. You cannot take the liberties that those born on the soil can. You must therefore insist on the comforts your body needs.

With love,

Yours,
Bapu

Gandhi to Miss Faering, [December 14] 1919[195]

Lahore,
Sunday [December 14] 1919

My dear child,

I have your letter and had the vest also. May I thank you for it? I am having it washed.

Have you commenced spinning? I would like you to study my article on *swadeshi* in *Young India.*[196] Will you please learn spinning and religiously give it one hour every day? Your and my forefathers wore only hand-spun and hand-woven clothing. The words spinster (from spinning) and wife (from weaving) are highly significant. I would like you to set an example to the ladies of the *ashram* in regular spinning. Is Fatima doing any now? If not please tell her and Amina not to neglect it.[197] They were to do it for a fixed time every day and so were all the ladies for that matter.

195. *My Dear Child*, pages 46-47; *Collected Works*, Volume 16, page 343.
196. "*Swaraj* in *Swadeshi*", *Young India*, December 10, 1919; *Collected Works*, Volume 16, pages 335-37. Gandhi wrote that the immediate problem before the country was to feed and clothe the people, because the purchase of foreign cloth was draining the resources. He suggested that spinning, weaving and other cottage industries be revived.
197. Fatima and Amina were daughters of Imam Abdul Kader Bawazir, an associate of Gandhi during the *satyagraha* in South Africa, who stayed in Gandhi's *ashram*.

I am glad they all nursed you during your illness. Mutual help and service is really the first step to a truly godly life.

With love,

Yours,
Bapu

[Gandhi wrote on January 13, 1920, to Miss Ada West, who had lived in the Phoenix Settlement, the *ashram* founded by Gandhi in South Africa:

"... Miss F[aering] should be able to live her own Christian life without the slightest hindrance in the *ashram*. I do expect you when-ever you find the time to pay us another visit and I hope that Miss F[aering]'s description of the beautiful surroundings in which we are living has but whetted your desire to visit us. I shall esteem it a privilege if you will give me your own impressions of Miss F[aering] both regarding her physique and her mentality. She is such a self-denying girl that I really sometimes do not know what she does want.

You will perhaps also be able to give me your confidence in this matter".[198]

Miss Faering went to Madras for Christmas. Gandhi wrote to Miss Anne Marie Petersen on January 13, 1920:

"... As soon as I heard that you wanted Miss Faering to join you during Xmas, I had no hesitation in saying that she should respond to your wish. I can thoroughly appreciate the Christian senti-ment that friends and relations should gather together and have sweet communion during the Xmas season. I must confess to you that Miss Faering's presence in the *ashram* is uplifting for us all. She is such a good-natured loving girl with all the loftiest aspirations that anyone can be capable of. We are all looking forward to meeting her again. I only wish that she will be able to keep her health here and become a better and a stronger Christian for her presence at the *ashram*. As I have so often told her, her living at the *ashram* can be justified only if she not only retains

198. SN7027; *Collected Works*, Volume 16, pages 475-76.

undimini-shed her Christianity but that, in the environment of the *ashram*, it becomes purer and more ref[ined] than ever before".[199]]

Gandhi to Miss Faering, [On or after January 16, 1920][200]

Delhi,
[On or after January 16, 1920]

My dear child,

I was sorry to leave the *ashram* as soon as you came. I wanted so to have a long chat with you and to comfort you if you were anxious about anything. I felt more sorry when Devdas told me you had not enough to cover yourself [with]. I hope you asked what you wanted or that someone anticipated your wants.

You know the changes that have been made regarding cooking. Bhuvarjee will be out of the kitchen. I would like you to help *Ba* in the kitchen. But you shall not do so if it costs overmuch patience. *Ba* has not an even temper. She is not always sweet. And she can be petty. At the present moment she is weak in body too. You will therefore have to summon to your aid all your Christian charity to be able to return largeness against pettiness. And we are truly large only when we are that joyfully. I have known friends being generous in a miserable spirit. Their generosity has become a kind of martyrdom. To rejoice in suffering, to pity the person who slights you and to love him all the more for his weakness is real charity. But we may not be able to reach that stage. Then, we should not experiment. And so, my dear Esther, if you find Mrs. Gandhi trying your nerves, you must avoid the close association I am suggesting to you. On no account shall I have you to lose your inward peace and joy. I want you so to order your life that the *ashram* gives you greater joy, greater happiness

199. SN7052; *Collected Works*, Volume 16, page 477.
200. *My Dear Child*, pages 39-40; *Collected Works*, Volume 16, pages 486-87

and finer perception of truth. I want you to be a greater Christian for being in the *ashram*. You were with me the whole of yesterday and during the night. I shall pray that you may be healthier in mind, body and spirit so as to be a better instrument of His service.

And I want you to befriend Deepak.[201] He is another big experiment. Mahadev will tell you who he is. I have not the time for writing more.

You may share this letter with Mahadev if you wish to. This has come to me in answer to prayer. Early this morning I wanted to send you a word of cheer. I feel for poor Mahadev just the same. He has an unequal burden to carry and thank God he has a most sensitive conscience that is unforgiving towards him. But he is fretful. He has not that abundant experience of the divine in him and so he worries. Help him please and derive help from him.

Write to me of your experience of your Madras visit and tell me how you felt there.

With deep love.

Yours,
Bapu

Miss Faering to Gandhi, January 20, 1920[202]

January 20, 1920

My dear *Bapujee*,

Your letter, which I received today was very dear and precious to me, as I myself felt it very much when I was not able to see much of you, before you just went away. But it was partly my own fault.

Ba is suffering from cold and fever, so I can do some little help here and there.

201. Sarladevi Chaudharani, a friend of Gandhi, had left her son Deepak at the *ashram*.
202. SN7066.

Yes, I have felt that it is difficult to please *Ba*; she may not know it herself, but I felt very often as if she did not like me to stay in the *ashram*. I asked her if I had done anything wrong, then I should correct it if possible, but I must feel happy with the people with whom I stay for everyday; I mean simply this kind of friendly fellow-feeling, which knits one together in sorrow as well as joys, but I fear *Ba* will always look upon me as a stranger and nothing more, although I have tried and will try to behave like a daughter, however poorly I can substitute a real daughter. She is kind in her heart and towards me too, but I find it difficult to cross the several barriers there seem to be between us, natural or unnatural. I am very willing to help her in the kitchen, when she is going to take that work, as I am now helping Burjubai but I am not quite sure whether she will accept my help.

Mahadevbhai is suffering very much, it pains me to look at him and see him so very downcast in his spirit. He asked me to write and tell you that you were always in his heart, and if your prayers were not able to give him relief from this horrid fever of his, he did not know any other help. I think he is not quite right in his point here; prayer, I am sure, can change God; but we are very short-sighted, and do not know what is best for us; only experience has proved that the finest characters are those who have been tested in the fire of sufferings, and therefore again can have sympathy with all who suffer; and those, who have glorified God most in this world is again those who cheerfully have suffered.

Mahadevbhai told me too, that he at the present time felt that he had no right or claim to live in the *ashram* when he so often fell ill. He asked me to write this too. But are we not all surrounded by limitations, we cannot always do that which we want to do; sometimes I think it is simply to teach us to depend more upon God than upon our own strength and power, but there is no greater trial or bitter disappointment than to feel that we are not able to lift the task we have put before ourselves; it means not only a spiritual defeat, but a humiliation in the eyes of the world. Does all this come into our lives to teach us about our utter helplessness? But we do need faith in ourselves and our cause in order to conquer.

I am happy in one way, but so many things from inside and outside is trying to rob our joy, and we must not allow anything to interfere with our joy, as true joy is our source of strength. But only yesterday I had a letter telling me that my only brother is dying, if not dead, suffering from a hopeless lung-consumption. He has been my childhood's dearest friend and playmate; yes, even in our first youth we shared everything. He is three years younger, the only son in the family, a clever promising man, but he had all his heart in this world and the manifold pleasures of life... is he taken apart, and shall leave everything and be quite alone. I wish in times like this of great sorrow that I could fly across to old Denmark, and see him at least once more. But no it is impossible. We must face all this when we once have made up our minds to leave our homes either for this or that reason.

I am taking Deepak in English lesson, he is a handsome bright boy very attractive but he finds it very difficult concentrate his mind even for a short time; but he is always ready to help and he is polite to everybody and at the same time a real boy always up to fun and a fight.

Bapujee, I have read your letter again and again, and how I love it; you are always thoughtful of others always forgetting yourself.

I want to write a longer letter, but it seems as if everybody today wants to disturb me and Manuben, that little pet is with me and requires some attention.

So I close this with all my love

from yours very thankful child

Esther

P.S. I need your prayers *Bapujee*, and I believe in prayer; they can work wonders.

I need strength—and joy—joy so I have more than just enough for myself.

I wish often, I was born in India.

Gandhi to Miss Faering, January 24, 1920[203]

Lahore,
January 24, 1920

My dear child,

I was delighted to receive your letter on my arrival in Lahore yesterday.

I am glad you have opened out your heart. It is the truest test of friendship and affection. You enable me to help you when you do open out. I had no notion that you had already observed Mrs. Gandhi's pettiness. I simply warned you, as I asked you to come in closer touch with her. As it is, my warning reached you just in time. God will give you wisdom and courage to do the right thing at the right moment. Only remember one thing, never allow your spirit of sacrifice to go to the length of making you sour and disgusted with yourself or your surroundings. This is one of the sorest temptations to which workers are exposed. They go on sacrificing themselves till they become disgusted with everything and everybody for want of response. We sacrifice truly only when we expect no response. It is well worth knowing the root meaning of the word. It means, as you might know, "to make sacred". We make neither ourselves nor others sacred when we are irritated or angry. There is often more sacrifice-sacred making-in a divine smile than in so-called substantial sacrifice. The instances of Mary and Magdalene[204] occur to me as I write these lines. Both were good but the one who simply waited upon her Lord without making any fuss was probably more self-sacrificing than the other. And so may it be with you. Do not overtax your spirit in trying to win over Mrs. Gandhi or anybody else. Immediately you find that you cannot get on with her, you must have a separate kitchen for yourself. You could still serve her but not be so intimate with her. Nothing that you do there should tire out either your spirit or your body.

203. *My Dear Child,* pages 47-49; *Collected Works,* Volume 16, pages 499-500.
204. This appears to be a slip for "Martha".

Do please ask for every convenience you may need whether for food or otherwise. Ask Maganlal or Imam Saheb[205] or anybody who has come nearer you.

Yes, Deepak is all you describe him. I would like you gently to get him to realise his responsibility and concentrate on his studies. Supervise his letter-writing. See that he writes fully and neatly to his mother every day.

My heart is with you in your sorrow. I can understand your desire to be with your brother in Denmark. But you have chosen a different path, a path that does not admit of exclusive service. May God give you strength for your task.

I agree with you about Mahadev. He is needlessly anxious about his health. He is prized not for his body but for his spirit. It must be a privilege for friends to nurse him in his illness.

With love,

Yours,
Bapu

Gandhi to Miss Faering, [January 25,] 1920[206]

Sunday, [January 25,] 1920

My dear child,

Narahari[207] tells me you are now boarding with Imam Saheb. I am glad you will certainly feel at home there more than anywhere else if only because you have someone who will talk to you constantly in English. And you can shower your discriminating love on Fatima with immediate results.

205. Imam Abdul Kader Bawazir, an inmate of the *ashram*. He had played a prominent role in the *satyagraha* in South Africa and served a term of imprisonment. Gandhi had high regard for him.
206. *My Dear Child*, pages 49-50; *Collected Works*, Volume 16, pages 506-07.
207. Narahari (or Narhari) Dwarkadas Parikh, an associate of Gandhi who helped manage the *ashram*.

I shall feel deeply hurt if you lose your health and your peace of mind. "Resist not evil" has a much deeper meaning than appears on the surface. The evil in *Ba*, for instance, must not be resisted, i.e., you or for that matter I must not fret over it or be impatient and say to ourselves, "why will not this woman see the truth or return the love I give her". She can no more go against her nature than a leopard can change his spots. If you or I love, we act according to our nature. If she does not respond, she acts according to hers. And if we worry, we "resist evil". Do you agree? I feel that that is the deeper meaning of the injunction. And so, in your dealings with everybody I want you to keep your equanimity. Secondly please do not deny yourself anything you may need for your bodily comfort. Ask me, if you will not ask anybody.

I want you to write to me daily whilst I feel uneasy about you.

With love and prayers,

Yours,
Bapu

[Shortly after, Gandhi wrote to Narahari Parikh: "...It does not matter if Miss Faering's meals have had to be arranged at Imam Saheb's... See that you look after Miss Faering as you do after Mahadev..."[208]]

Gandhi to Miss Faering, January 26, 1920[209]

Lahore,
January 26, 1920

My dear child,

I have your brief note. I hope you have been receiving my letters regularly. I have hardly missed a day. I cannot send you a love-letter today as I have not many minutes for the post.

208. SN11883; *Collected Works*, Volume 16, page 510.
209. *My Dear Child*, page 49; *Collected Works*, Volume 16, page 512.

How is Deepak shaping? Please tell Deepak he has not written to Sarladevi for the last 4 days. He must be regular in writing.

Please see that he writes at least a p[ost]c[ard] every day.

Yours,
Bapu

Gandhi to Miss Faering, January 29, 1920[210]

January 29, 1920

My dear child,

I passed two days by without writing but not without thinking or talking of you. Your health is not what it should be. You may not be able to digest *chapati*.[211] You should then take the usual loaf. Anasuyabehn will bring it for you. Tell Imam Sahib about it. And you may take milk in the morning with some fruit and bread and *dahi*[212] in rice for breakfast, with some vegetables simply boiled. Perhaps the *dal*[213] may not suit you. Thus a little bread, a little rice, a little vegetable and *dahi* may be your breakfast. In the evening too it may be this. And a little fresh fruit, an orange, say, at noon; whether this is proper or something else you will finally decide. Only you must put your body right even as an artisan's first duty is to keep his tools in order. God has given us this body as a tool to be used efficiently for His service, neither for pampering nor for keeping in cotton wool but not even for abusing or spoiling it by neglect. This is a wretched sermon but much needed.

With love,

Yours,
Bapu

210. *My Dear Child*, pages 51-52; *Collected Works*, Volume 16, page 520.
211. flat bread made of wheat flour.
212. yogurt.
213. a lentil dish.

Gandhi to Miss Faering, [January 30, 1920][214]

Friday [January 30, 1920]

My dear child,

No letter from you today. I am surrounded by too many people who want me, to be able to write to you a love-letter. I therefore send you my prayers and all love.

Yours,
Bapu

[PS.]

Do give me a cheering and cheerful letter if you can.

M. K. G.
Friday

[Gandhi wrote to Narahari Parikh around this time:

"I have been a little concerned on hearing that Miss Faering has gone to Lilavatibehn's. Miss Faering is a very simple-minded girl. She puts trust in everyone all too readily. Lilavatibehn will befriend her for unworthy purposes. So let me know in more detail what happened and why she went. If anyone makes unworthy approaches to her, it would be a matter of shame for us. Do not talk about this. I have dropped a hint to Maganlal and do so to you".[215]]

Gandhi to Miss Faering, [February 1,] 1920[216]

Lahore,
Sunday [Morning, February 1,] 1920

My dear child,

You have been a bad child to keep me without a line for so many days. I do however hear about you from others. You are at a

214. *My Dear Child,* page 54; *Collected Works,* Volume 16, page 521.
215. SN11888; *Collected Works,* Volume 16, pages 522-23.
216. *My Dear Child,* pages 54-55; *Collected Works,* Volume 17, page 3.

marriage party. I have felt a little disturbed. What is it all about? How could you have fared in the midst of strangers? It was wrong if you went as a matter of duty. For no duty lay on you to attend such parties. If you went for the sake of a change I don't know that you had a desirable change. Where was the party? What were the people? Did they know English? What was your food there? Where did you have to sleep? Who suggested your going? It seems all so strange to me. I do not want you to make experiments in the dark. It is early Sunday morning and I am filled with anxiety about you. I know it is stupid to be anxious. God is above us all to protect and guide His own. But you give me the privilege of calling you my child. "Rock of ages, cleft for me; let me hide myself in Thee".

With deep love,

Yours,
Bapu

[Gandhi wrote to Narahari Parikh around February 1: "Esther has made a big mistake in leaving. I have repeatedly written to her and Maganlal. If she, of her own accord, shows my letters, you will find all of them worth reading". (SN11886)]

Gandhi to Miss Faering, [February 1, 1920][217]

Lahore,
Sunday [February 1, 1920]

My dear child,

The enclosed[218] was written in the morning. I have just got your pencil letter. I do clearly see that you made a mistake in accepting the invitation. You are young, you are in-experienced. You have a golden heart but it needs steadying. What is a big ship without a rudder? Where does it go? Does it not drift? My heart

217. *My Dear Child*, pages 55-56; *Collected Works*, Volume 17, pages 3-4.
218. The previous letter of the same date; see above.

weeps for you today. You have left a surrounding[219] where you could grow after a fashion; you have come to a surrounding[220] where you can grow much more if you will assimilate the surrounding. You must not prick yourself in your waywardness. A disciplined conscience is one to obey. It is the voice of God. An undisciplined conscience leads to perdition, for the devil speaks through it. I wish I was with you. "Not everyone that sayeth unto me Lord, Lord, shall enter the kingdom of heaven, but he that doeth the will of my Father which is in heaven shall enter that kingdom". I am quoting from memory but it will do.

Do put yourself under discipline. Never do anything without consulting Maganlal. Let him be as elder brother to you. Come close to him. Ask for the food you need, take the rest you want and put your mind and body at rest.

Write to me daily a full letter.

I shall pray for you and love you all the more for your waywardness.

Yours,
Bapu

[Gandhi wrote on the same day to Maganlal Gandhi:

"There is a letter from Esther and hence I write this second letter to you. I have written to her as well. She made a great mistake in going.[221] I can see her weakness. This is how a holy soul falls. She claims too much independence. She feels humiliated to have to ask anyone. She is like a ship without a rudder. She has a large heart, but does not know what to do with it.

"I have advised her in my letter that she should look upon you as an elder brother and obey you, discuss matters with you. You should see her and find out her needs. If necessary, she may

219. The Danish Mission in south India.
220. the *ashram* at Sabarmati.
221. to attend a marriage party.

stay with you. It is possible that, by herself, *Ba* will not be able to look after her. I so much want to be in the *ashram* at this time. My heart is bleeding. It does not seem that Esther has done anything sinful. But I also believe that she may do such a thing in no time. This feeling may be only an expression of my fear".[222]]

Gandhi to Miss Faering, [February 4, 1920][223]

Wednesday [February 4, 1920]

My dear child,

I have your letters. It is no use crying over spilt milk. How to mend matters now is the question. You shall certainly go where you wish during Easter or any time. Your mental and spiritual happiness is the primary consideration. For the irregularity you mention there is a sovereign remedy tried by L. K.[224] It consists in hip and friction baths and a diet without salt and other condiments. We have the book at the *ashram*. Read it. S. K. and others know it. *Ba* also has tried them for a number of years with the best of results. Do try them whilst you are there. Please don't hesitate to get bread. It is such a simple thing to procure.

I agree with you that you should have a quiet time and spiritual communion. Why will you not go to the church in Ahmedabad? But this is not suggested in the place of the convent. God will guide you and give strength and light.

With prayers and love,

Yours,
Bapu

222. *Collected Works*, Volume 17, pages 4-5.
223. *My Dear Child*, pages 52-53; *Collected Works*, Volume 17, pages 12-13.
224. Louis Kuhne.

Gandhi to Miss Faering, [February 5, 1920][225]

Lahore,
Thursday [February 5, 1920]

My dear child,

I see I have hurt you; forgive me. I wrote as I did because I love you so. I am afraid it is no use your coming here, because I shall be touring from the 11th.[226] So I cannot be with you even if you come. I hope to be with you on the 23rd at the latest. And we shall have some time at least together. Meanwhile please take the hip and the Sitz baths. And why will you not be examined by the doctor who is there? If I were you I should have no such compunction. But I don't wish to press you.

With prayerful love,

Yours,
Bapu

Gandhi to Miss Faering, [February 8, 1920][227]

Sunday [February 8, 1920]

My dear child,

I have seen your pathetic letter to S.[228] I am glad you have poured out your heart in it. I have telegraphed to you today asking you not to leave [the *ashram*] before I reach if you can at all stay. I want to have a few long chats with you in the early morning which I get only at the *ashram*. I could urge you too to have the baths I have suggested. Ask for the water to be brought to you.

Are you an unworthy child? You have made yourself dearest to me by your wonderful love and conscientiousness. You do not

225. *My Dear Child,* page 57; *Collected Works,* Volume 17, pages 13-14.
226. Gandhi was on tour in the Punjab from February 11 to February 15.
227. *My Dear Child,* pages 56-57; *Collected Works,* Volume 17, page 20.

for one moment think that your waywardness can make any alteration in my estimation of your worthiness. It is my privilege to point out where you need strengthening. If the body is the temple of the Holy, it requires the utmost care-certainly not pampering but equally certainly not disregard or even indifference.

With deep love always mingled with prayer,

Yours,
Bapu

Gandhi to Miss Faering, [February 10,] 1920[229]

Lahore,
Tuesday [February 10,] 1920

My dear child,

I have your dear telegram and two letters in one day. I had telegraphed before I received your letter about your father. I am sure that you should answer that call by going [to Denmark] as early as possible. Only I want to have many a chat with you before you go. Never mind the weakness of body today. I would like you still to consider the *ashram* as your home to which you could return whenever you wished to. If you feel like going now to Madras and come back on your way to Denmark you may do so. But I prefer seeing you before you go to Madras. But pray do whatever is in your opinion best. Take warm baths and you will get rid of the rash. The hip baths must do you good.

I want Devdas to go with you. I shall discuss it with him and with you when we meet. The idea of Mahadev going attracts me more.

D.[230] has a little book given to him by a missionary. It is called *The Inner Shrine*. In a hymn I read these lines: "With

228. possibly Mrs. Sarladevi Chaudharani, a friend of Gandhi, in Lahore.
229. *My Dear Child*, pages 50-51; *Collected Works*, Volume 17, page 22.
230. possibly Devdas Gandhi.

happy grief and mournful joy, /My spirit now is filled", and at once I thought of you. "Happy grief" and "mournful joy" are wonderful expressions. But no more today.

With love and prayer,

Yours,
Bapu

Gandhi to Miss Faering, [February 12,] 1920[231]

Thursday [February 12,] 1920

My dear Esther,

You and Mahadev are foremost in my mind as I finished my mouth wash. I have detained you in Ahmedabad. But have I done right? If your health grows worse where am I? I therefore want you to await me only if you keep at least tolerably well. Otherwise we must meet on your return from Madras. Please don't consider yourself bound to stay on because I have expressed the wish. To express purest love is like walking on the edge of a sword. "None of self and all of Thee" is easier sung than practised. We never know when we are not selfish even when we fancy we are all love. The more I think of it, the more I feel the truth of what I have often said. Love and truth are two faces of the same coin and both most difficult to practise and the only things worth living for. A person cannot be true if he does not love all God's creatures; truth and love are therefore the complete sacrifice. I shall therefore pray that both you and I may realise this to the fullest measure.

Yours,
Bapu

231. *My Dear Child*, pages 53-54; *Collected Works*, Volume 17, page 26.

Gandhi to Miss Faering, [February 15, 1920][232]

On the train to Benares,[233]
Sunday [February 15, 1920]

My dear child,

I am on my way to Benares and we shall soon meet. How I wish you were with me serving me like Devdas. I know you would love it and so would I. No man can supply the place of father but I would like to be that to you to the extent of my ability in this land of your adoption. I feel humiliated at the thought of your having to go to Denmark to recuperate yourself. Nothing would please me better than to send you to Denmark fully restored to health and a fuller Christian and a fuller daughter. And you have all the possibilities in you of a full growth in this life. May God grant you all your dearest wishes and may He make you an instrument of great service to humanity. Your love for India can only be acceptable as an expression of your love for humanity. "None of self and all of Thee" is a big prayer, [the] biggest of its kind.

May it be true of you and me.

With all love,

Yours,
Bapu

[Miss Faering's health deteriorated and she left for south India to recuperate before Gandhi's return to the *ashram*.]

232. *My Dear Child*, page 58; *Collected Works*, Volume 17, page 35.
233. Now Varanasi.

Gandhi to Miss Faering, [February 22, 1920][234]

The *Ashram*,
Sunday [February 22, 1920]

My dear child,

I found three love letters from you awaiting me on my return today. I was delighted to note the air of cheerfulness, quiet resignation and trust in God in your letters. The latter you always had in you. But your letters show deeper trust. May your trust go deeper and deeper still till at last you are freed from all doubt and therefore are all joy whatever happens. For as we go forward in our journey of life, we have always problems coming up for decision and they are the hardest when the voice of Satan nearly approaches the voice of God. Only fullest trust and perfect purity and extreme humility can lead us to the right choice.

I hope to be at the *ashram* for at least a week and then hope to seek solitude and rest for a fortnight.

I shall certainly miss you tonight at the time of retiring.

With love,

Yours,
Bapu

[PS.]

You will be glad to learn that S. 's father has returned your watch. The value lies not in the return but in the motive behind it. You will take it when you return on your way to Denmark.

Bapu

234. *My Dear Child,* page 59; *Collected Works,* Volume 17, page 43.

Gandhi to Miss Faering, [March 3,] 1920[235]

Bombay,
Wednesday [March 3,] 1920

My dear child,

The case is going on,[236] and as I have a few minutes' interval, I want to give you a few lines.

You are constantly in my mind. Sometimes I even feel uneasy when I think of our chats and when I think that in some things I might have appeared harsh when I had wanted to be gentle. One's speech cannot be judged by one's intentions but only [by] the effect it produced on the hearer. Are you happy and joyful? How are you in body?

I would like you to return Mr. Banker's[237] trunk. If you need another, you may take one in Madras. You will let me have your programme, of course.

The case is finished and the judgment has been reserved. I have sent you a telegram.[238]

With love,

Yours,
Bapu

Gandhi to Miss Faering, March 14, 1920[239]

[The announcement of the betrothal of Miss Faering to E. K. Menon, a Hindu, resulted in a storm of criticism

235. *My Dear Child,* pages 66-67; *Collected Works,* Volume 17, page 67.
236. Gandhi and Mahadev Desai were charged with contempt of court for an article in *Young India.* They were reprimanded by the High Court on March 12.
237. Shankarlal Banker, an associate of Gandhi.
238. This telegram is not available.
239. *My Dear Child,* page 60; *Collected Works,* Volume 17, pages 89-90.

from Hindus, as well as Christians. Gandhi wrote this, and the ten letters, which followed, to console Esther Faering.]

The *Ashram*,
March 14, 1920

My dear child,

Of course I will pray and I know I can do no better. Friends can help you little during the crisis you are passing through. May God protect you.

Once to every man and nation
Comes the moment to decide,
In the strife of Truth with Falsehood,
For the good or evil side.
Some great cause, God's new Messiah,
Offering each the bloom or blight,
Parts the goats upon the left hand
And the sheep upon the right
And the choice goes by for ever,
Twixt the darkness and that light.

I hope to pick out something like this, if I can, every day, charged with my prayers. What I have sent you today is from Lowell.

With love,

Yours,
Bapu

[PS.]

My case is decided. The court I understand has reproved us both but no penalty.

Bapu

Gandhi to Miss Faering, March 16, 1920[240]

Bombay,
March 16, 1920

More things are wrought by prayer
Than this world dreams of.
Wherefore let thy voice
Rise like a fountain for me night and day.
For what are men better than sheep or goats
That nourish a blind life within the brain,
If knowing God they lift not hands of prayer
Both for themselves and those who call them friend?
For so the whole round earth is every way
Bound by gold chains about the feet of God.

Tennyson

My dear child,

The above is my share in your sorrow for today. May it lighten your burden.

With love,

Yours,
Bapu

240. *My Dear Child*, page 61: *Collected Works*, Volume 17, pages 90-91.

Gandhi to Miss Faering, March 17, 1920[241]

Bombay,
March 17, 1920

Teach me, my God and King,
In all things Thee to see,
And what I do in anything,
To do it as for Thee,
All may of Thee partake,
Nothing can be so mean
Which with this tincture, 'for Thy sake,'
Will not grow bright and clean.
A servant with this clause
Makes drudgery divine;
Who sweeps a room as for Thy laws
Makes that and the action fine.
This is the famous stone
That turneth all to gold;
For that which God doth touch and own
Cannot for less be told.

George Herbert

241. *My Dear Child*, page 62; *Collected Works*, Volume 17, page 93.

My dear child,

May there be some line, some word, some thought to soften your grief.

With love,

Yours
Bapu

Gandhi to Miss Faering, [March 18, 1920][242]

Bombay,
Thursday [March 18, 1920]

Lord, it belongs not to my care
Whether I die or live;
To love and serve Thee is my share,
And this Thy grace must give.
If life be long I will be glad
That I may long obey;
If short, yet why should I be sad
To soar to endless day?
Christ leads me through no darker rooms
Than He went through before;
He that unto God's kingdom comes
Must enter by this door.
Come, Lord, when grace hath made me meet
Thy blessed face to see;

242. *My Dear Child*, page 63; *Collected Works*, Volume 17, page 95.

For if Thy work on earth be sweet,

What will Thy glory be?

My knowledge of that life is small;

The eye of faith is dim;

But 'tis enough that Christ knows all,

And I shall be with Him.

Richard Baxter

My dear child,

Another evening has come to fill me with thoughts of you. I pass them to our common Maker to make of them such use as He will for your good.

With love,

Yours
Bapu

Gandhi to Miss Faering, [March 19, 1920][243]

Bombay,
Friday [March 19, 1920]

Oh I could go through all life's troubles singing,

Turning each night to day,

If self were not so fast around me, clinging

To all I do or say.

My very thoughts are selfish, always building

Mean castles in the air,

I use my love of others for a gilding

To make myself look fair.

243. *My Dear Child*, page 64; *Collected Works*, Volume 17, page 98.

I fancy all the world engrossed with judging
    My merit or my blame.
Its warmest praise seems an ungracious grudging
    Of praise which I might claim.
Alas! no speed in life can snatch us wholly
    Out of self's hateful sight,
And it keeps step, whene'er we travel slowly
    And sleeps with us at night.
O Lord that I could waste my life for others,
    With no ends of my own,
That I could pour myself into my brothers
    And live for them alone.

My dear child,

You have forgotten your promise. Do not keep me without anything from you for so many days. The above is my selection for the day.

With love,

Yours,
Bapu

Gandhi to Miss Faering, March 21, 1920[244]

Sunday, March 21, 1920

I say to thee, do thou repeat
    To the first man thou mayest meet

244. *My Dear Child*, page 65; *Collected Works*, Volume 17, page 108.

In lane, highway or open street-
    That he and we and all men move
Under a canopy of love,
    As broad as the blue sky above;
That doubt and trouble, fear and pain,
    And anguish all are shadows vain.
That death itself shall not remain,
    That weary deserts we may tread
A dreary labyrinth may thread,
    Through dark ways under ground be led,
Yet, if we all one Guide obey,
    The dreariest path, the darkest way
Shall issue out in heavenly day;
    And we on diverse shores now cast,
Shall meet, our perilous voyage past,
    All in our Father's house at last.

Trench

My dear child,

I am on the train to Delhi. I could not go out for rest.[245] I sent you nothing yesterday. I could not. This may be my last for some days because I shall not know what will happen from day to day. Do let me have a line from you.

With love,
Bapu

245. Gandhi was advised rest as he had some trouble with one of his legs. In the last week of March and again at the end of April he went to Sinhgadh for rest.

Gandhi to Miss Faering, [March 22] 1920[246]

Monday [March 22,] 1920

My dear child,

Here is my selection for today:

He that is down needs fear no fall
He that is low, no pride,
He that is humble ever shall have
God to be his guide.
I am content with what I have
Little be it or much
And Lord! contentment, still, I crave
Because Thou savest such.
Fullness to such a burden is
That go on pilgrimage.
Here little and hereafter bliss,
Is best from age to age.

J. Bunyan

With love,

Yours,
Bapu

Gandhi to Miss Faering, [March 25] 1920[247]

[Miss Faering decided to leave for Denmark and wished to meet Gandhi before catching the boat in Bombay.]

246. *My Dear Child*, page 66; *Collected Works*, Volume 17, page 109.
247. *My Dear Child*, page 67; *Collected Works*, Volume 17, pages 292-93.

[Delhi] Thursday [March 25,] 1920

My dear child,

My heart and my prayers are with you. Your letter grieves me beyond words. That you should suffer so much pain! But true joy will come to the godly. And as my faith in your godliness is unshakable, I have a certain belief that you will have a peace full of joy.

You will certainly see Mr. Menon if you think that you should. I am anxious for you to get an early boat. The voyage will give you the solitude you need and your home and your father the comfort and the companionship you will want.

If you have not returned Mr. Banker's trunk, please do not send it by parcel. It may be returned on your coming back to Bombay. There is absolutely no hurry.

With love,

Yours,
Bapu

Gandhi to Miss Faering, March 30, 1920[248]

On the train,
March 30, 1920

My dear child,

I have just received your letter for which I thanked God. I am from a resting place going to the *ashram*. After leaving Delhi, I have not been able to write to you. I had four days' good rest.[249] I hope to go back after the 13th April. When are you going to Denmark?

With love,
Bapu

248. *My Dear Child*, page 68; *Collected Works*, Volume 17, page 298.
249. Gandhi left Delhi on March 25 and was at Sinhgadh from March 26 to 30.

Gandhi to Miss Faering, April 15, 1920[250]

Sabarmati,
April 15, 1920

My dear child,

I have just returned from Bombay. I passed the fasting and prayer week[251] at Bombay. It is true I have not written to you but that does not mean that I have thought any the less of you or prayed for you less lovingly. I had no time and I felt I had sent you enough verses to last you for some time. I should send more if I knew your condition of mind. And so I allowed a few days to pass by without committing myself to writing.

But now I have your precious letter. I am quite resigned to your marriage. I will not argue against it. You will do exactly as God guides you. Only always be sure it is the voice of God.

Yes, I should certainly love to see Mr. Menon. That you are willing to give yourself to him is proof enough to me that he is no ordinary young man.

There is no certainty about my going to London. It is mere talk as yet; I have written to the Viceroy and much will depend upon the answer.[252]

I had very rich experiences in Bombay during the fasting week. But of these when we meet. When are you likely to leave for home?

With love,

Yours,
Bapu

250. *My Dear Child*, pages 68-69; *Collected Works*, Volume 17, pages 315-16.
251. The Indian National Congress from April 6 to April 13 observed national Week.
252. Gandhi was pressed to go to England to acquaint the government and the public about the strong feelings in India about the rights of the Muslim countries and control of their holy places. But he decided at the end of April 1920 not to go.

Gandhi to Miss Faering, May [2,] 1920[253]

Sunday, May [2,] 1920

My dear child,

I do not know whether you have arrived [in Bombay]. If you have, do come up to Sinhgadh.[254] It is a beautiful place. It is reached from Poona by a *tonga*.[255] If I knew, I could easily arrange everything. But I know you are able to manage this yourself. Sinhgadh is about 13 miles from Poona. The *tonga* hire is at least Rs. 5/-. Sometimes it is more.

With love,
Bapu

[Miss Faering accepted Gandhi's invitation and reached Sinhgadh on May 3.]

Gandhi to Miss Faering, May 9, 1920[256]

The *Ashram*,
May 9, 1920

My dear child,

I did not at all like to part with you. But I know it was good for your health's sake. I only hope that the expectation has been fully realised and that the climate of Sinhgadh has agreed with you.

I am sorry there is no chance of my being with you as early as I had thought. The great strike commenced today.[257] I, however,

253. *My Dear Child*, page 69; *Collected Works*, Volume 17, pages 376-77.
254. Gandhi stayed in Sinhgadh from April 29 to May 4.
255. horse carriage.
256. *My Dear Child*, pages 69-70; *Collected Works*, Volume 17, page 402.
257. Workers in the textile mills in Ahmedabad went on strike under the guidance of Gandhi.

do hope that it will not last long. The mill-owners have no case and they have no fighters in their midst. It was a big meeting last night. The men were full of courage and determination.

I cannot help writing down for us again the heavenly lines of Trench :

Yet, if we will one Guide obey

The dreariest path, the darkest way

Shall issue out in heavenly day;

And we on diverse shores now cast,

Shall meet, our perilous voyage past,

All in our Father's house at last.

With love,

Yours,
Bapu

Letter from Gandhi, May 16, 1920[258]

The *Ashram*,
May 16, 1920

My dear child,

I cannot send you a love-letter, for the publication of the peace terms[259] again unsettles the regularity of my work. I am glad you are able to leave quite so early as the 19th.[260] I hope you received

258. *My Dear Child*, pages 70-71; *Collected Works*, Volume 17, page 425.
259. Peace terms presented by the Allies to Turkey. Gandhi was at this time leading a national movement in defence of Turkey and the Caliphate (*Khilafat*).
260. Miss Faering left for Denmark on *S.S. Berlin* on May 19, 1920. Gandhi could not see her again before her departure.

my telegram[261] in reply to yours. Please do not worry about what happens to us here. We are all in God's keeping and if we wait upon Him and Him alone, whatever happens is for our good. Even so-called afflictions turn out then to be for our benefit. Give yourself perfect rest and peace at home, let your father meet you as a better Christian for having been to India and having come in contact with the *ashram* and then when you are rested, strong in body, mind and soul, return.

May you have a safe voyage, a happy time at home and a safe return. You will write of course regularly and give me your home address.

With deep love,

Yours,
Bapu

Gandhi to Miss Faering, May 21, 1920[262]

Ashram,
May 21, 1920

My dear child,

I tried to overtake you on Wednesday, but it was not to be. I had to settle the dispute of labour. I therefore postponed. They all told me you were anxious to meet me. Of course you were. A friend is waiting to take the post, so I must be brief. I have your last precious letter. I know you will be all you say. May God bring you back safe, strong in body, mind and spirit.

I hope you received my note on the *Berlin*.

Yours,
Bapu

261. This telegram is not available.
262. *My Dear Child*, page 71; *Collected Works*, Volume 17, page 438.

Gandhi to Miss Faering, June 25, 1920[263]

Bombay,
June 25, 1920

My dear child,

I have not been regular in writing to you as I had intended to. I have been too busy with the *Khilafat* question. I did however ask Mahadev to write to you on my behalf. You must also be receiving *Young India* regularly.

I had expected to hear from you from on board. But as yet there is nothing from you. I wrote to you a letter to reach you on your steamer[264] and another to London care of Thomas Cook. I do hope you received both these letters.

I am now fixed up for the time being in Bombay. I enclose herewith the letters to the Viceroy.[265] They will give you an idea of my activity. Devdas is with me.

I am anxious to hear about your meeting with your father and your health. Of course I expect to hear from you regularly.

With love,

Yours,
Bapu

Gandhi to Miss Faering, [September 2, 1920][266]

On the way to Calcutta, [September 2, 1920]

263. *My Dear Child*, page 72; *Collected Works*, Volume 17, pages 511-12.
264. Presumably the "note" referred to in the letter of May 25.
265. Presumably his letter of June 22, 1920, to the Viceroy explaining why he had advised non-co-operation with the British Government unless the peace terms for Turkey were revised; and a letter on the same day to the private secretary to the Viceroy enclosing a representation by Muslims on the same subject.
266. *Collected Works*, Volume 18, page 223.

My dear child,

I had your first long letter from home. I was delighted.

I had four very pleasant days with Menon. He is frank, honest and clean. He is unassuming. I have invited him to come to the *ashram* any time he likes. I have told him too that both you and he could stay at the *ashram* and make it your home there.

He has still difficulties. Pressure is being put upon him to own Christianity for your [sake].[267] I consider that unworthy of both of you. Your religion must be above everything. It is not a mechanical thing to be changed at will. Therefore in my opinion you must keep your respective faiths.

Then what about your children if you decide to bear them? It is a tremendous question for a godfearing person.

The solution I can see is that though you may marry, you may not see each other carnally. But you will both do as God directs you. Menon wished me to write to you what we talked and I have done. The solution appealed to him then. But that signifies nothing. Your connection is too sacred to tamper with.

Anne Marie, that is Miss Petersen, [as she] insists on my calling her, [and] I have fallen in love with each other. Of course I had nothing to forgive. But I must not describe the interview. She must have done it.[268]

Ba, Devdas, Mahadev, Imam Saheb, Shankerlal Banker, Anasuya Behn are with me among many others. These however you know. Harilal[269] I shall meet tonight in Calcutta.

I know you are spreading there love for India. May God bless you and your mission.

With love,

Yours,
Bapu

267. The original has "case", evidently a slip.
268. Please see text of letter by Miss Anne Marie Petersen to Gandhi in 1920.
269. Gandhi's eldest son.

Gandhi to Mrs. Menon, September 4, 1921[270]

[This letter was written after hearing the news of the marriage of Miss Faering with E. K. Menon in Denmark.]

On tour,
September 4, 1921

My dear Esther,

I found your letter awaiting me on my return to Calcutta from the East Bengal tour.

I wish you and yours a happy life of service.

I was longing for your letter and to hear how you were doing.

I cannot understand your not getting *Young India*. I am inquiring.

When you return to India, you will find the *ashram* devoting its best time to carding, spinning and weaving. I wish you would study Danish hand-spinning, hand-weaving, if there be any such in Denmark.

God is great. Not by the effort we are making, but by His grace it is possible to gain *Swaraj*[271] this year. And then you return without hindrance.[272] There will be just as much steadfastness needed to work out *swaraj* as is needed for attaining it. Let Anne Marie work here for its attainment and you will work there to make it a success.

With love to you both,

Yours,
Bapu

270. *My Dear Child*, pages 73-74; *Collected Works*, Volume 21, pages 58-59.
271. *Swaraj* (*Swarajya*)—self-government, independence.
272. The British Government refused her permission to return to India, but she returned in December without hindrance.

Gandhi to Mrs. Menon (telegram), January 11, 1922[273]

[The Menons returned to India and were helping Miss Anne Marie Petersen with her school and *ashram* at Porto Novo.]

Sabarmati,

January 11, 1922

GOD BLESS YOU BOTH.

GANDHI

Gandhi to Mrs. Menon, February 5, [1922][274]

February 5, [1922]

My dear child,

I have your welcome letter. You were certainly right in your attitude. Let the Government do what they choose. Please keep me informed of what goes on. At this stage I am not publishing the news. As you see I am in Bardoli preparing for mass civil disobedience. You must have read my letter to the Viceroy.[275]

With love to you all,

Yours,
Bapu

273. *My Dear Child*, page 74; *Collected Works*, Volume 22, page 155.
274. *My Dear Child*, page 74; *Collected Works*, Volume 22, page 337.
275. On February 1, 1922, Gandhi wrote a letter to the Viceroy explaining the decision to launch mass civil disobedience in Bardoli in protest against "repression of a virulent type".

Gandhi to Mrs. Menon, March 8, 1922[276]

Ajmer,
March 8, 1922

My dear child,

It is only here where I have come for a day, that I get the time to write to you. The loss of your Bohemian independence is more than made up by your sharing your life with another. If marriage has any meaning at all, it must point to the greater self-surrender which is in store for everyone of us.. The surrender by two dissimilar (in form) persons one to the other is greater independence because it is a realisation of greater responsibility. The discharge of the greatest responsibility is the greatest independence. This is secured only by the fullest surrender to God.

I know you will come whenever you can. I am not moving from Gujarat for some time, if I am still left free. There are all sorts of rumours about my arrest.

Miss Petersen owes me a letter.

With my love to you all,

Yours,
Bapu

Gandhi to Mrs. Menon, March 17, 1922[277]

Sabarmati Jail,
March 17, 1922

276. *My Dear Child*, page 75; *Collected Works*, Volume 23, page 23.
277. *Speeches and Writings of M. K. Gandhi*, page 747; *Collected Works*, Volume 23, page 99.

My dear child,

Well, I hope you were all happy over the news of my arrest.[278] It has given me great joy, because it came just when I had purified myself by the Bardoli penance[279] and was merely concen-trating upon no experiment but the proud work of *khaddar*[280] manufacture, i.e., hand-spinning.[281] I would like you to see the truth of the spinning-wheel. It and it alone is the visible outward expression of the inner feeling for humanity. If we feel for the starving masses of India, we must introduce the spinning-wheel into their homes. We must, therefore, become experts and, in order to make them realise the necessity of it, we must spin daily as a sacrament. If you have understood the secret of the spinning-wheel, if you realise that it is a symbol of love of mankind, you will engage in no other outward activity. If many people do not follow you, you have more leisure for spinning, carding or weaving.

With love to you all,

Bapu

278. Gandhi launched a non-violent non-co-operation movement in August 1920 in protest against brutal repression in India and the violation of promises by Britain to Indian Muslims concerning Turkey and the Caliphate. He was arrested on March 10, 1922, and was sentenced to six years' imprisonment on a charge of sedition. He was, however, released on February 5, 1924, when he fell ill.
279. Suspended the movement. He then fasted in penance from February 12 to 17, 1922.
280. *Khaddar* (or *Khadi*), handspun and hand-woven cloth.
281. On February 12, the Working Committee of the Indian National Congress decided to launch a "constructive programme" which included, as one of the main activities, hand-spinning and manufacture of *khaddar* as a means to counter massive unemployment, underemployment and poverty in the country.

Mrs. Menon to Gandhi (telegram), January 16, 1924[282]

[Gandhi, then imprisoned in Yeravda Jail, was operated on January 12, 1924, at Sasoon Hospital for appendicitis. He was released from prison on February 5.]

CUDDALORE

MAHATMA GANDHI

POONA HOSPITAL

POONA

ALL LOVE SYMPATHY AND PRAYERS FOR YOUR RECOVERY LONGING TO SEE YOU AGAIN *BAPUJEE*

YOUR CHILD

ESTHER

Mrs. Menon to Devdas Gandhi[283], *January 21, 1924*[284]

Porto Novo
January 21, 1924

My dear Devadas,

When I read about *Bapujee's* operation[285] my first thought and desire was to take the first train to Poona and see *Bapujee* again after nearly four long years: but you know I have a baby now, nearly a half a year old, and just now she is not well. She has

282. SN 8131.
283. Youngest son of M.K. Gandhi.
284. SN8195.
285. Gandhi was operated for appendicitis on January 12, 1924, and was in the Sasoon Hospital in Poona until February 5 when he was unconditionally released from prison.

for some ten days had a very persistent bad stomach trouble, so I have to nurse her day and night.

But tell *Bapujee* that I am longing and praying for the day I can again fall at his feet and get his blessing for me and the baby.

I am happy beyond words because *Bapujee* will be restored again to us.

Our hearts are rejoicing because we know *Bapujee* will bring back to us the message, which only can give India a future and a hope.

God is great, He can use also disease in order to carry out His will and purpose. No message of love and sympathy could come inside the prison walls, and our letters were returned and our hearts were often troubled and full of anxiety for *Bapujee's* sake, and we felt the burning shame and humiliation because *Bapujee* was in prison and suffering for our sake and at the same time against the wish and will of the nation.

Again shall the torch of truth burn in our midst and the flame of love and passion for service search our hearts and inspire them to deeds.

Again shall we hear the voice ringing with peace and the message of universal brotherhood between man and man.

Again shall *Bapujee's* smile gladden our hearts, the smile which opens the bud of the human heart so love bursts forth like when the sun swirls and shines upon the flowers so they blossom with sweet fragrance.

We thank and praise God our Father for all what *Bapujee* has meant and is to us.

We thank him even for the lesson given to us through *Bapujee's* imprisonment.

The lesson which taught us in the most vivid and living way that love and love, and nothing but love can conquer the hearts of man, and that we only live through self-sacrifice.

Devadas, tell *Bapujee* that a tiny wee baby is longing for the day *Bapujee* will take her in his arms and dedicate it to service for Mother India.

My heart is full of joy, and could fill pages and pages with a child's joy and rapture and delight when father returns home after a long journey.

It is singing in my soul because we shall again be with *Bapujee*, who better than anybody else has lifted our hearts above the things which will vanish and perish. Let us all thank God for this everlasting loving goodness and faithful hands which bent over *Bapujee* also in prison.

All love to all of you, to *Bapujee* and *Ba* from

Esther *Bahen*

Mrs. Menon to Gandhi, September 30, 1924[286]

United Theological College
Bangalore
September 30, 1924

My dear *Bapujee*,

I don't deserve that you ask about me: where I am. I have been so faithless since I left Poona,[287] and I ask for your forgiveness.

I wanted to write to you when I came down to Madras, but when I (was) there received a letter from Tagore telling us that they had got another doctor there instead of my husband. Then I remembered your words about the *ashram*, which was still open for us, if we did not get on in Santiniketan, and as soon as my husband came down to Madras, I talked with him about the possibility of going to the *ashram*.

My husband who will never take any step in a hurry said we shall wait and see before we decide anything. God must have something to show us since He has prevented us from going north and I am in a critical period, where I need quietness of mind.

286. SN10232.
287. Mrs. Menon visited Gandhi in Poona on the eve of his release from prison in February 1924.

I did not talk more to my husband about this matter but I did not know what to write to you although I daily said, "we must write to *Bapujee*". Time went on and one day my husband told me that he desired to be baptised and he added, "I have now the same ideal, and I am for Christ. Why should I not then work together with Anne Marie when we already have shared nearly four years in sorrow and joy". This happened in the beginning of March and I should then have written to you but I felt a pang of pain in my heart because we in one way have our heart in your *ashram*, but we feel also we are one with Anne Marie in our service for India and we have stood side by side during hard times.

Now I have told what I should have written months ago.

My husband is (of) a very reserved nature and he finds it difficult to write to you, to whom he looks up with the reverence and love the son has for his father and the disciple for his *Guru*.

But since you have done more for me than any father could do for his child, I ought to have written long ago to you. It is your birthday on the 2nd of October according to our calendar.

You don't care for empty words or any promise which will not be kept. We do desire to serve India and work for her; and we know also what you want us to do.

We will daily pray God to give us the will and the strength to serve India in the way you have told us. We believe in it, and it is my disease which often has been in my way.

May the New Year also bring the fulfillment of your heart's desire and deepest prayer, unity of mind, of heart amongst all Mother India's many children.

Your sufferings and penance for our sake and your love is bound to bear rich fruit.

Our little girl, who is now a little over a year old, can say "*Bapujee*" with her sweet little voice. Every morning she looks at your photo and says: "*Bapujee*".

Yes, on her half-year's birthday, when she was taken in your arms and blessed by you, she was also dedicated to the service of India.

I believe it will gladden your heart to hear that when we have morning prayer here in the college the English professor is praying to God for your health and strength to carry out your purpose for the good of India and that God may still grant you many years to live for the service of India.

I follow your wonderful letters and messages we get in *The Hindu*.

I know God, who is a God who can work wonders, will carry you through your fast,[288] because He has a future and a past and a hope for India which is linked up with your service for India; and if we lost you now, we would have to work without hope for India because she had killed her own soul.

And God still has the best in store for India as a nation.

With love and prayers from

Baby Nanni and your child Esther

Gandhi to Mrs. Menon, October 5, 1925[289]

October 5, 1925

My dear Esther,

I am writing this at Deoghar which is a beautiful place in the Bihar tour. Today is my Monday.[290] I have your long letter before me. I have always thought of you all. I was much relieved to know that you had completely recovered and that the recovery was due to an Indian medicine. I hope that, having regained your health you will keep it.

288. Gandhi was on a fast in Delhi for 21 days from September 17 to October 8, 1924, for Hindu-Muslim unity, as riots between Hindus and Muslims had taken place in several cities and towns.
289. *Collected Works*, Volume 28, pages 291-92.
290. Gandhi observed a day of silence on Mondays.

It is good that Miss Petersen is to go to Denmark early next year. She deserves the rest. It is nice too that she will leave the school in a progressive state. I had no doubt about its success. Patience was all that was needed. In these days of many bogus or selfish things, people look askance at anything new or out of the ordinary.

Are you also at Porto Novo? Or has Menon got something after his heart?

Of course, you are all coming into the Spinners' Association.[291] Have you read the constitution?

I had a very sweet letter a month or two ago from a Danish lady. I would certainly love to go to Denmark. But [I] have no desire to leave India until non-violence is more firmly rooted than it is in the soil. I know that it is truth, but I may be a poor representative of it. This I know that I cannot live without truth and non-violence.

If you take up the task of writing my biography,[292] you have to pass many months at the *ashram* and, may be, even travel to South Africa and visit Champaran and Kheda, probably the Punjab, too. It is a big job if it is done thoroughly. It was in these places I tried to work out non-violence as I understand and know it.

With love to you all and kisses to baby,

Yours,
Bapu

[PS.]

I reach the *ashram* in the beginning of November.

291. Gandhi set up the All India Spinners' Association in 1925.
292. She published a biography of Gandhi in Denmark in 1930.

Gandhi to Mrs. Menon, December 11, 1925[293]

Wardha,
December 11, 1925

My dear Esther,

I was looking forward to hearing from you for a long time. I was therefore delighted to hear from you. I am glad you are better.

You have heard all about my fast?[294] I am none the worse for it. I have almost regained the lost weight in ten days and am now resting with J.[295] at Wardha.

Miss Slade whom we call Mira is with me and is coming to the Congress.[296] She was glad to get your letter. She will write to you, I expect, if she has not done so already.

I hope to return to the *ashram* about New Year's Day.

M.[297] has lofty ideas of service. May they all be realised!

Is the school growing? How many children-boys and girls- have you? What is your syllabus?

With love to you all,

Yours,
Bapu

[PS.]

I am here till 21st instant.

293. *My Dear Child*, page 77; *Collected Works*, Volume 29, page 312.
294. Gandhi undertook a fast from November 24 to December 1 because of misconduct in the *ashram*.
295. presumably Mr. Jamnalal Bajaj, an associate of Gandhi.
296. Miss Margaret Slade, daughter of Admiral Sir Edmund Slade of Britain, became interested in Gandhi and joined his *ashram* in 1925. Known as Mira or Miraben (Mirabehn), she was closely associated with him until his death.
297. presumably Miss Anne Marie Petersen.

Gandhi to Mrs. Menon, February 10, 1926[298]

Ashram, Sabarmati,
February 10, 1926

My dear child,

I have your letter and I have the parcel too from Menon. There are no directions in the parcel beyond saying that there is a powder as an opening medicine and the contents of the bottle are for malaria. So far as I am myself concerned at the present moment, I am free. If I get a renewal of the attack I do not know that I can take the medicine, for as you are aware, I can take only five ingredients during any 24 hours whether for food or for medicine.[299] Most of these Ayurvedic medicines contain dozens of ingredients. Therefore, however useful they may be in themselves, for me they are perfectly useless. But so many people get malaria here and I would gladly try Menon's remedy if I get the directions. Please, therefore, ask him to send them to me and if he knows the ingredients, he may give me an idea of them.

Now about Friendship. You have used the word "friend" in three different senses. If we have the capacity, we can all become friends as Jesus was. There, the word "friend" means a kind helper. The friendship between ourselves and those who are superior to us is also a one-sided thing. A father is and should be his children's friend. There it becomes companionship with the good, *satsanga* as it is called in Sanskrit. What I have written about is intimacy between two or more persons, where there is no secret and where mutual help is the consequence of, not a motive for, friendship. The motive is some indefinable attraction. It is this exclusive relationship which I have considered to be undesirable and antagonistic to communion with God.

Such was the friendship between the person I have described in the Autobiography and myself.[300]

298. *Collected Works*, Volume 29, pages 453-54.
299. This was a vow of Gandhi.
300. In Part I, Chapters VI and VII, of the autobiography, which had been published in *Young India* on January 21 and 28, 1926, Gandhi described his friendship at school with Sheikh Mehtab who had persuaded him to eat meat and caused him to be cruel to his wife.

Does not spinning naturally interest you? I should expect you, if you spin at all, to spin because you are interested in it. And if you are interested, you should master the mechanism and keep your instrument in perfect order as you will keep your stove in order if you are interested in cooking.

Spinning for me is an emblem of fellowship with the poorest of the land and its daily practice is a renewal of the bond between them and ourselves. Thus considered, it is for me a thing of beauty and joy for ever. I would rather go without a meal than without the wheel and I would like you to understand this great implication of the wheel. If you are to spin at all, I do not expect you to take up the wheel simply because I commend or the Congress recommends or because it is likely to be of economic value.

I am daily picking up strength little by little.

With love to you all,

Yours,
Bapu

Mrs. Esther Menon

Porto Novo (S.I.R.[301])

Gandhi to Mrs. Menon, April 30, 1926[302]

Ashram, Sabarmati,
April 30, 1926

My dear child,
I have your letter. I do feel disturbed about your health. You must regain your original freshness and strength.

I am sorry to hear about the disorganisation of Miss Peterson's school. I have not received any yarn yet from the girls referred to

301. South Indian Railway.
302. *My Dear Child*, page 80; *Collected Works*, Volume 30, pages 384-85

by you. You can have as much *khaddar* rags as you want and soft used *khaddar*.[303] If you tell me what length you require I shall see to it being sent. It is difficult to fix any price for used *khaddar*. You will therefore either send what you can or not at all. You will not stint yourself in anything for the sake of paying for the *khaddar* that you may order nor will you on this account hesitate to ask for the exact quantity you want. I am glad that Menon is helping poor patients in the way he is doing.

What does it matter so long as you make both ends meet and it need not matter even if one cannot make both ends meet in acts of service.

Andrews reaches Bombay tomorrow.

Yours,
Bapu

Gandhi to Mrs. Menon, June 23, 1926[304]

The *Ashram*,
Sabarmati,
June 23, 1926

My dear child,

I have your letter. Now you know everything about the much talked of visit to Finland.[305] I felt that the time had not yet arrived for going. I could see no clear definite light. Undoubtedly, had I gone to Finland, I would have gone to Denmark also. I had made that definite promise to Anne Marie and I would have loved to have seen your own home. But that was not to be.

Mirabai is doing quite well and she is standing the heat wonderfully well. I am glad you have a helper. You have not yet

303. for nappies for the new baby.
304. SN19632; *My Dear Child*, page 81; *Collected Works*, Volume 31, page 39.
305. Gandhi had been invited to the World YMCA Conference in Finland. He considered a visit to Finland and Denmark, but decided against it.

told me what sort and what quantity of old *khaddar* is to be sent to you. But Maganlal has made a parcel. It is being despatched today to the address given by you at "Craiglea". I suppose "Craiglea" is the name of the cottage in Kodaikanal. It is quite like Menon that he should be devoting himself to the care of the sick. You refer to Rs.[306] 10/-. Nothing has been received here as yet. Nothing need be sent.

Yours,
Bapu

Mrs. Esther Menon

"Craiglea"

Kodaikanal[307]

Gandhi to Mrs. Menon, July 16, 1926[308]

The *Ashram*,
Sabarmati,
July 16, 1926

My dear child,

I have your letter. Why must you enter into all the explanation in respect of Rs. 10/-? I would be grieved if you pinch yourself for sending me Rs. 10/-or anything. As there was a question in the *ashram* as to whether the money was received or not and whether, if it was received, it was mislaid, I told you about it. But, it would please me better if you will keep the *khaddar* and not think of paying for it. After all, what has been sent to you is second-hand *khaddar* from old stock belonging to the members of the *ashram*. Nor need you hesitate to ask for more if you want more.

306. Rupees.
307. Kodaikanal is a hill station and summer resort.
308. *My Dear Child*, page 82; *Collected Works*, Volume 31, pages 148-49.

I am delighted to hear of the progress made by Nani.[309] It would be an achievement if she speaks three languages equally well when she grows up. I suppose, the strong will she inherits from her mother and gentleness from her father, or, will you say *vice versa?*

It is too early to think of what I shall do next year. But, if I do come to the South, I would love to go to Porto Novo.

With love to you all,

Yours
Bapu

Mrs. Esther Menon

(Porto Novo)

S. I. R.

Gandhi to Mrs. Menon, August 8, 1926[310]

The *Ashram*,
Sabarmati,
August 8, 1926

My dear child,

I have your letter. At least at the top of it you have my own writing and, for the time being it should be enough. I too detest the typewriter. I have a horror of it, but I survive it as I survive many things which do not do lasting harm. If someone dispossessed me of the typewriter, I should not shed a single tear, but, as it is there, I make use of it and even believe that some time is being saved for more useful work. But, even in this belief, I may be totally wrong. It is so difficult to rise superior to one's surroundings always.

309. Esther Menon's daughter, Nan (or Narayan).
310. *My Dear Child*, page 83; *Collected Works*, Volume 31, pages 280-81. This is one of the few typed letters sent by Gandhi to Mrs. Menon.

Evidently Anne Marie is doing great and good work.[311] Prejudices die hard! But, wherever there is earnestness, there is no difficulty about breaking down the hardest prejudices.

It will be a nice thing when Menon has his own hospital. Mirabehn wanted to go through 7 days' fast as a spiritual experience. She completed it this morning and broke it on fruit juice. She took the fast extremely well though she has lost ten pounds in seven days. But that of course is nothing.

I do not expect much from the Viceroy. He may be well-meaning, but mere good intentions count for little. But as you have very properly guessed, I can only say, whether it takes long or short, salvation must come only through ourselves.

Yours,
Bapu

Mrs. Esther Menon

Porto Novo

Gandhi to Mrs. Menon, August 20, 1926[312]

The *Ashram*,
Sabarmati,
August 20, 1926

My dear child,

I have your letter. I did not misunderstand your remark about typewriters. On the contrary, I liked it.

The literal meaning of an "*ashram*" is an abode, but the associations about the *ashram* are these: It should be simple. It should not be merely a teaching institution. It should contain predominantly those who are pledged to perpetual continence. It should have associations of *sannyasa*, meaning detachment from the world. It should, therefore, be a voluntarily poor organisation.

311. Miss Petersen was then in Denmark.
312. *My Dear Child*, pages 84-85; *Collected Works*, Volume 31, pages 318-19.

There should, therefore, be rigid simplicity about it. Its object must invariably be formation of character with a view to self-realisation. The idea of master and servant is wholly repugnant to such an institution. All men and women in an *ashram* are expected to do bodily labour and all enjoy an equal status. The idea of superiority has no place in it. The head of an *ashram* is in the place of a parent and he is expected to regard the rest as his own children. I wonder if I have now given you fairly the characteristics of an *ashram*.

It grieves me whenever I find that a medical man is weak or ailing. It is a perpetual reminder to us that medicine is such an incomplete, such an unreliable, and such an empirical science. If we think about it with sufficient detachment, we would at once realise its inherent weakness by understanding that there is no such thing as an absolute cure. The most potent drugs admit of innumerable exceptions. The most successful operation leaves literally and in the spirit a scar behind. It would certainly be a good thing, if you could hasten your departure for Denmark. Change of climate will be the best cure.

What you say about fasting is quite true. It has no absolute value and it certainly does not produce the slightest spiritual effect if the motive behind it is not really spiritual. Fasting with a mixed motive ends with purely material results. But fasting for the sake of unfoldment of the spirit is a discipline I hold to be absolutely necessary at some stage or other in the evolution of an individual. I always considered Protestan-tism to be deficient in this particular. Every other religion of any importance appreciates the spiritual value of fasting. Crucifixion of the flesh is a meaningless term unless one goes voluntarily through pangs of hunger. For one thing, identification with the starving poor is a meaningless term without the experience behind. But I quite agree that even an eighty days' fast may fail to rid a person of pride, selfishness, ambitions and the like. Fasting is merely a prop. But as a prop to a tottering structure is of inestimable value, so is the prop of fasting of inestimable value for a struggling soul.

With love,

Yours,
Bapu

Gandhi to Mrs. Menon, September 17, 1926[313]

The *Ashram*,
Sabarmati,
September 17, 1926

My dear child,

The Roman Catholic fast which you refer to in your letter is really no fasting at all, but there is or there was a real fast also amongst them. However, whether they have or they had or not is of no consequence to us. Neither fasting nor anything else that is imposed from without can be of any value. You need not have apologised for raising the question about Christ. In spite of most devout attention to every word ascribed to Jesus in the New Testament and in spite of my having read in a humble spirit all about Jesus, I have really not seen any fundamental distinction between him and the other great teachers. That you see a vast difference between Jesus and the other teachers I can understand, explain and appreciate. That is the teaching you have imbibed from childhood and you would read everything else with that unconscious conviction. Nobody taught me in my childhood to differentiate. I have therefore grown without bias one way or the other. I can pay equal homage to Jesus, Muhammed, Krishna, Buddha, Zoroaster and others that may be named. But this is not a matter for argument. It is a matter for each one's deep and sacred conviction. I have no desire whatsoever to dislodge you from the exclusive homage you pay to Jesus. But I would like you to understand and appreciate the other inclusive position.

What Menon has told you about the pecuniary difficulty is quite correct. But so is your remark. You will come here if God makes the way clear for you.

Yours,
Bapu

Mrs. Esther Menon

Porto Novo

313. *My Dear Child*, pages 85-86; *Collected Works*, Volume 31, pages 419-20.

Gandhi to Mrs. Menon, [October 27, 1926][314]

[Sabarmati,
October 27, 1926]

My dear child,

My blessings on the addition to the family.[315] Hope you and the baby are steadily progressing. Any of the names suggested by you is good. The shorter the better.

Yours,
Bapu

Gandhi to Mrs. Menon, [before March 26, 1927][316]

[Before March 26, 1927]

My dear child,

I have your pathetic letter. I was wondering why there was nothing from you so long. Now I know. It distresses me to find you in such a dilapidated condition.[317] I am writing this in the midst of distractions. I have not a moment to spare. I therefore send you my love and prayerful blessings. I am in the South in April. I must make a desperate effort to meet you during the tour.

When Maria returns I must see what can be done for spinning.[318]

With love to you all,

Yours,
Bapu

314. *My Dear Child*, page 79; *Collected Works*, Volume 31, page 533.
315. birth of the second daughter, Tangai.
316. *My Dear Child*, page 87; *Collected Works*, Volume 33, page 194.
317. She had become ill, apparently because of the climate.
318. Miss Petersen returned from Denmark in 1927.

Gandhi to Mrs. Menon, February 18, 1928[319]

[The Menons left for Denmark in 1927. Dr. Menon went from there to England for further studies and the family joined him there in 1929.]

The *Ashram*,
Sabarmati,
February 18, 1928

My dear child,

I had your two letters under one cover. It did appear to me that you had forgotten me entirely, and yet I knew that that wasn't possible...[320] was looking a picture of health when I saw her at Madras, and she told me all about you.

You must have heard about the relapse in my health.[321] I am now under strict orders not to do any serious work involving mental or physical strain. Except for spinning, therefore, I am on my back. I am dictating this whilst spinning. But there is no cause for anxiety. I am getting better and hope soon to be allowed to move about.

Yes. The *ashram* remains what you have seen it to be. The population is daily increasing and we have too few houses to accommodate all the inmates.

I am asking for a complimentary copy of *Young India* to be sent to your address, and I shall see that as many back numbers as can be spared are also sent.

I am so glad that all of you are flourishing in health. What is Menon doing in England? Please send my love to him when...[322] whom you know is in the *ashram* just now.

319. SN14241; *Collected Works*, Volume 36, pages 32-33.
320. The original is damaged here.
321. Gandhi fell ill on February 5.
322. The original is damaged here.

She has come to pass a few days on her return from Delhi where she had gone to attend a women's conference. Mirabai is here and keeping very good health indeed.

With love,
Bapu

Mrs. Esther Menon

14 Asylvej

Taarbaek, Denmark

Mrs. Menon to Gandhi, March 21, 1928[323]

Taarbak
March 21, 1928

My dear and wonderful *Bapuji*!
I have just received your letter.

I am sorry to hear about your illness. But it is no wonder since you always are overworking your-self. No other mortal could stand the strain you put upon yourself for the sake of others.

My husband is trying to take the L.M.S. and the L.M.M. in two years. So he has to study very hard. But he will come to Denmark during his vacation in August and September. And we are looking forward to that time.

When I ask Nani, if she has forgotten her father, then she says, "No he looks brown and has black hair".

Both my children are having a very hard attack of whooping cough and Nani has, says the doctor, cranial malaria, and too big liver and spleen, it came up together with the cough with high fever every third day.

So during the last month I have had little or no sleep in the nights and I have lost two lb. My weight is only 92 lb.

323. SN14269.

I shouldn't bother about my weight, if I did not feel terribly tired always.

No strength, no will.

It has now been decided in the Radio Council that I shall give three lectures about you, in Radio.

(i) Gandhi as I have seen him

(ii) Gandhi and his influence in or upon India, and

(iii) Gandhi's *ashram* school

I am a little nervous about speaking in the Radio; I like to face somebody and catch their attention, if I at all have something so say.

Things are moving rapidly in India, (as) I understand from the papers.

Thank you very much for letting me have a copy of "*Young India*".

I can hear your voice, when I read your articles. How I should love you to come to dear, old Denmark, when the beach is green and the meadows full of flowers and soft grass and the clear water playing everywhere at all our seashores in small waves.

But what would you like to see in Denmark, I wonder.

Fine cows! Cooperative Societies, folk high schools, farms and what more!

Who will accompany if you come?

Devadas and Mahadevbhai?

They both deserve a trip to Europe for they have shared everything with you and ever since Mahadevbhai was very ill of typhoid fever he did need a real change of air.

My Indian *khaddar* towels, sheets etc. are often admired here in Denmark and people say they would like to buy *khaddar* from India. But I believe that would not be the right thing to do or in accordance with your views of *Swadesi* to send *khaddar* out of India.

Your postcard in answer to my wire came today.

Thanks! I shall eagerly be looking forward to the great event of your coming to Europe.

I hope, we will be ready for your message, and that you will not be too disappointed with us.

All love your old child

Esther

Mrs. Menon to Gandhi, May 20, 1928[324]

May 20, 1928

My dear and wonderful *Bapuji*,

It was a matter of great sorrow to me, when I in *Young India* read about Maganlalbhai's death.[325]

Never shall I forget, when I met him for the first time in the old *ashram*, and since then he was during my stay in the *ashram* like an elder brother.

He had a rare lustre in his beautiful eyes as an expression for a pure and noble soul.

If *Bapujee* those first days in your *ashram* still lingers in my heart with all its freshness and sweetness, they belong to my most sacred and treasured memories in life.

And later, when I stayed in the *ashram*, I came again in close contact with Maganlalbhai.

324. SN14315.
325. Maganlal, a nephew of Gandhi, was manager of Gandhi's *ashram*. He died on April 23, 1928.

He was always serving everybody at his ..., and he spared no effort in order to make me feel comfortable in the *ashram*.

I remember him at the evening prayer and at the work and in his beautiful, little house near the riverbank. He gave me his advice as well as his help.

I remember how you wrote to me "Esther, you must put yourself in discipline. Now you have the advantage of Maganlalbhai's advice in the *ashram*".

Still now, when I am getting older, I regret this lack of discipline in my life. I am at present in bed getting-treatment, injections for veins on both legs. The first week everything was alright, I was getting better, but then all on a sudden they became worse, hard and painful and a big boil appeared on the one leg and the doctor told me to get ... and keep quiet.

I was again impatient and left my bed and walked and the result is I am much worse.

For several months I have been engaged in writing my lectures about you.

I have now given two on radio, and they were received well.

I know that if there was anything in them beautiful it is you, who have inspired me and it has been a great joy for me to deliver those lectures. I feel still the meeting with you has been the greatest event in my life.

You are in fact my ideal. Your love and care for individuals is unsurpassed and that's why you can love the nation so well.

Bapujee! I wish, God will grant me to meet you again. Your photo taken before the long fast is hanging over my bed.

I understand very well, it would be a terrible strain on you to come to Europe.

And yet, why could not Romain R[olland] say, that you should come to Europe because we need you here much more than we stand in need of a personality like Rabindranath Tagore.

When I read the lines "For European Friends", I did not feel like any who belong to that class.[326] My home is India and my children are Indians although little Nani or Narayan (her real name) said she wants to stay in Denmark, because she burns her feet on the sand in India. Both children are strong and healthy after nearly two months...

My husband will be coming to Denmark in July, and we three will be happy.

Nani wonders already, why I have not got brown skin like her father.

Mr. Gregg's book on *khaddar*[327] is very interesting and startling indeed.

We are only now getting summer in Denmark, with all its sunshine and flowers and a blue sky.

I could not for a moment think of you in European dress, that ugly stiff dress; indeed your outward form is an expression for the inward form.

Nani asks when she looks at your photo: Is *Bapujee* very poor?

All love yours

Your affectionate child

Esther

PS. My address is Hove
pr. Asnaes
Denmark

We will then hope and pray that the year 1929 will see you in Denmark.

326. Gandhi wrote an article entitled "To European Friends" in *Young India* (April 26, 1928) explaining his decision not to travel to Europe that year. *Collected Works*, Volume 36, pages 266-68.
327. Richard B. Gregg, an American, stayed in Gandhi's *ashram* for a year. He wrote *Economics of Khaddar*, *Power of Nonviolence* and other books on Gandhian thought.

Gandhi to Mrs. Menon, June 22, 1928[328]

Satyagraha Ashram,
Sabarmati,
June 22, 1928

I have your two letters. Maganlal's death has not only upset all my plans but has prompted me to make what may appear revolutionary changes in the *ashram*. I must not therefore give you a long love-letter.

If all goes well and the friends in Europe still want me, I hope to find myself in readiness to go next year.

I can understand your being ill in India, but why should you be ill there? I expect you to return with your original bloom and vigour.

How long do you both expect to be away? Where is Menon studying?

Mrs. Esther Menon
Have, Asnaes
Denmark

Gandhi to Mrs. Menon, October 12, 1928[329]

Satyagraha Ashram, Sabarmati,
October 12, 1928

My dear child,

I had your letter after a long lapse of time. It was therefore doubly welcome. I hope that this finds you in better health and that if there was an operation that it was quite successful and has left no ill effects.

328. SN14336; *Collected Works*, Volume 36, page 450.
329. SN14411; *Collected Works*, Volume 37, page 358.

The *ashram* is undergoing many changes at the present moment. You will see them all described in the pages of *Young India* when the time comes.[330] Except for malaria which is seasonal for this time of the year, everything goes well here.

Remember me to Menon when you write to him.

Mrs. Esther Menon

Gandhi to Mrs. Menon, January 25, 1929[331]

The *Ashram*, Sabarmati,
January 25, 1929

I have your letters, including the one you gave to the Danish sisters.[332] They were here for over a week. They left only two days ago and they told me they enjoyed their stay at the *ashram*. They had their meals at the common board at which over 175 men, women and children sit.

Maria has written me that you are still weak and have not completely recovered after your operation,[333] but that you and Menon are due to return at the end of the year. I shall be glad to see you both and the children face to face.

330. Gandhi wrote in *Young India* (November 4, 1928) that all the inmates of the *Satyagraha Ashram* at Sabarmati had not succeeded in observing its rules regarding truth, celibacy, nonviolence etc., interpreted strictly. It was therefore decided to maintain the *ashram* as an ideal, but to run all its external activities (e.g. industries to help poorer classes) in the name of "*Udyog Mandir*". The *ashram* would keep for itself a small ground for prayers.
The managing committee of *Udyog Mandir* decided to stick to the rules of the *ashram* but to treat them as ideals toward the fulfilment of which every member would constantly strive.
An experiment was also being made of running a single kitchen for the entire *ashram*. *Collected Works*, Volume 38, pages 22-24.
331. SN15130; *Collected Works*, Volume 38, page 400.
332. Mrs. Ellen Horup and Miss Cathinca Olsen.
333. for appendicitis.

Nothing is yet decided about my European visit this year. But I am hesitating especially in view of the Congress resolution.[334] Maria says I can best go to Europe as a messenger from a free India.[335] My reason inclines towards that view, but I am waiting on God for light.

Yours sincerely,
Mrs. Esther Menon

Taarbaek, Denmark

Mrs. Menon to Gandhi, June 18, 1929[336]

14 Asylvej,
Taarbaek
June 18, 1929

My very dear *Bapujee*,

It is a long time since I have heard from you but I know you are working and always working for the liberty and freedom of our own Mother India. My only wish and prayer for the New Year is that God's great and wonderful plan with you may be fulfilled to His glory and for India's sake.

May you have the joy to see *Swaraj* throughout India before your next birthday.

And–without any bloodshed and bitterness.

We have had a very fine summer and my husband was here in Denmark during his vacation.

We do hope to return some time next year for India.

334. In December 1928, the Indian National Congress adopted a resolution, moved by Gandhi, that if Britain did not grant dominion status to India within a year, non-violent non-cooperation would be revived.
335. Please see letter from Miss Anne Marie Petersen to Gandhi on January 15, 1929.
336. SN11827.

I enjoy my reading of *Young India*, which enables me to follow things out in India even from a distance.

We had the privilege to meet Professor Karve[337] and other prominent men from India during the International School Congress.

What a pity you could not be there.

I wonder when you will give Denmark the joy and privilege to be here.

You can see how our children grow.

All love.

Your old child

Esther

Mrs. Menon to Gandhi, undated [1929][338]

14 Asylvej, Taarbaek
Denmark

My very dear *Bapujee*,

I am so sorry I never congratulated you with the splendid result of the Bardoli campaign although it often has been in my thoughts.[339]

Bardoli has proved worthy of your great trust; that gives also hope for the future.

Not everybody will be able to see success in one's own lifetime.

337. Prof. D. K. Karve (1858-1962), educator and social reformer.
338. SN15129.
339. In 1928, farmers in Bardoli district protested against an increase in land tax of more than twenty percent and asked that an impartial tribunal consider the matter. When the Government refused, they began a no-tax campaign under the guidance of

I have ... left the hospital, also I have been operated for appendicitis; that was the first time I have been operated.

I liked to be in the hospital in one way.

I felt thankful for every little loving service shown to me by the nurses, and I became familiar with suffering and death in a more intimate way, than I do when I am out in the rush of life. I learnt in another sense the truth of the words: "Measure thy life by loss instead of gain, not by the wine drunk but the wine poured forth. For love's strength standeth in love's sacrifice and whoso suffers most hath most to give".

We have now gone back to Taarbaek, one of the most beautiful suburbs of Copenhagen near forest and the seashore, and here will we stay, until we go back to India.

It is too long a stay in Europe in many ways; the children feel at home here and are used to our climate. They love the snow and the rain(?) alike.

I have just read your articles in *Young India* about *ahimsa.*[340] Oh! for a pure delight to read them, so clear and so bold in its expressions and views; how much we could learn from them, if we have an open mind, and if we are humble enough to revise our own ideas of *ahimsa*.

And I read with still greater joy your article called "God is".[341] Every word of it speaks to my heart and confirms my own ... experience about God.

Yes, "the purer I try to become the nearer I feel to be to God". I too feel it to be true *Bapujee*, but I find it difficult to be good.

Gandhi. The Government resorted to arrests, seizure of land and livestock, and other repressive measures, but the farmers stood firm and were supported by public opinion all over the country. The Government was obliged to compromise. On August 6, 1928, it reached an agreement releasing prisoners and restoring property. An inquiry board was appointed and it recommended that the tax increase be reduced to about six percent.

340. *Collected Works*, Volume 37, pages 338-41, 381-86, 408-11.
341. *Collected Works*, Volume 37, pages 347-50.

I mean not to be selfish and half-hearted in my daily life or cold and indifferent to others' sufferings.

I have been asked to give a lecture about your *ashram*. I wish I could wait, until I have read about all the changes it has undergone now. But they want it now for the radio; so I must use my memory, as I go right back to the first time when I had the great privilege to meet you on the 6th of January 1916.[342]

I have been asked also to give a lecture in the academic association about "The Ideas and Ideals of India contra those of the West". That is rather a big theme, and I hope I shall do credit to India also here. I have learnt a lot from you, when I shall deal with this subject.

C.F. Andrews article in *Young India* called "A Land of *Rishis*" is simply charming;[343] if all Englishmen were just a little more like this saint, there would be no race feeling or ill-will between India and England.

My husband is working hard, he will be glad to see your letter. He will spend about a week during Xmas and New Year with us three here in Denmark.

We are longing back to India and we must hope our long stay in Europe has been for the good and made us still more fit to serve Mother India in the best way.

With love and prayers,

Your child Esther

P.S. May I get a copy of the book, *Self-Restraint vs. Self-Indulgence*?[344]

342. This should be 1917.
343. This article by C.F. Andrews about a visit to the Marburg University in Germany was published in *Young India* on October 21, 1928. An Indian student, referring to the Sanskrit scholars at the University, said: "Oh, Mr. Andrews, this is a 'Land of *Rishis*'".
344. Book by Gandhi.

It might be good to translate it as a means to work against all the forces for evil in connection with the sexual life here in Denmark.

Gandhi to Mrs. Menon, June 7, 1931[345]

As at Sabarmati,
June 7, 1931

After having kept me waiting for many long months you have at last written to me. What a bad thing that Menon has not yet got his diploma. I had a letter from a mutual friend saying that you were disheartened over this failure. This is unworthy of you as I have known you. No failure, no adversity should dishearten you who have a living faith in God and his goodness. We do not know that every failure is a matter for sorrow nor do we know that every adversity is an infliction. Do we not often find that prosperity and success mean the undoing of people whereas failure and adversity chasten them?

I do not know that I am going to London. If I do, I will of course love to go to Denmark and if I went there I should not like to miss you. But it is no use speculating on a highly problematical thing.[346]

I do hear from Maria, now and again.

After dictating this I came upon another letter which mentions you more intimately. This letter is from Dr. Henning Dalsgaard.[347] In that letter he says you are cheerful but he asks

345. SN17254; *Collected Works*, Volume 46, page 350.
346. Gandhi went to London in 1931to attend the Round Table Conference on constitutional reform in India. He visited Birmingham and met the Menons.
347. Dr. Dalsgaard was lecturer in Political Science at International People's College in Elsinore.

me whether I can do anything for Menon. I do not however find any concrete proposition. Have you any such in view? If you have, you will not hesitate to tell me and of course if I can do anything, you know also you can rely upon my doing it.

Mrs. Esther Menon
M, Quest House
Selly Oak
N. Birmingham (England)

Gandhi to Mrs. Menon, January 21, 1932[348]

[Gandhi was detained in Yeravda Central Prison from January 4, 1932, to May 8, 1933. He wrote several letters to Mrs. Menon and her children from prison.]

Yeravda Central Prison,
January 21, 1932

My dear child,

Your account of the meeting with the ailing sister[349] is touching. Give my love to her when you visit her again.

I hope you are at peace with yourself now. The children must be quite well. Kiss them for me if they will let me kiss them.

Maria was with me in Bombay. But I had hardly time to talk to her.

348. *My Dear Child*, pages 87-88; *Collected Works*, Volume 49, pages 15-16.
349. Nellie Ball, an English girl, poor and bed-ridden, who was a great admirer of Gandhi.

I hope Menon is doing well. My love to him and to all at Woodbrooke settlement.[350] Send my love to Miss Harrison[351] and tell me where she is staying. Do you write to Maud Cheeseman?[352]

Love.

Bapu

[PS.]

Sardar Vallabhbhai is with me.[353] Both of us are doing quite well.

Gandhi to Mrs. Menon, February 28, 1932[354]

Y.C.P.[355]
February 28, 1932

My dear child,
I was delighted to have your letter again and the unexpected scribble from Nani.

I see you have a cosmopolitan company.[356] I only hope this does not give you more than your health can manage.

350. The Quaker Centre, near Birmingham. Mr. and Mrs. Menon were closely associated with it. Gandhi had visited it in 1931.
351. Miss Agatha Harrison, a Quaker. She met Gandhi in India in 1929 and assisted him during his visit to London in 1931. At Gandhi's suggestion, she worked for reconciliation between India and Britain.
352. Mrs. Maud Cheeseman, sister of Henry Polak, was associated with Gandhi in South Africa and assisted him during his visit to London in 1931.
353. Vallabhbhai Patel, an associate of Gandhi who led the *satyagraha* in Bardoli, was detained with Gandhi. He was Deputy Prime Minister of India after independence.
354. *My Dear Child*, pages 88-89; *Collected Works*, Volume 49, page 165.
355. Yeravda Central Prison.
356. "The Menon home at Selly Oak was always an international centre". (*My Dear Child*, page 88).

No, the *Gita* does not teach differently. What it does teach is that all our acts must be natural and spontaneous even when unconscious. When they are so, there is no thought of reward or result. There is, therefore, in pure love no giving and no taking. Put in another way there is no giving on earth without taking. Love gives because it must; it is its nature. It therefore does not calculate whether there is a corresponding gain. It is unconscious of the giving and more so of the taking. Love is its own reward. When there is that ineffable love, there is a joy which is above all the so-called joys we think we experience from outward circumstances. It is that joy I want you to possess. There was a time when you thought, I thought, you had it. But you had not then gone through the fire. The joy that will surely be yours one day will come out of the purifying richness of that fire. It will steal over you when it does come. May it come soon.

We are both well.

Love.

Yours,
Bapu

Gandhi to Nan Menon, February 28, 1932[357]

Y.C.P.
February 28, 1932

My dear Nan,

Your attempt to write a letter to me was very good. And what a reindeer you have sent. What lovely horns! I am sorry I am not playing with the goats, though they are brought before me everyday twice to be milked. I don't play because when they come, I am always doing something which I must not give up. Yes, there are a few flowers but nothing much to speak of. The ground

357. *My Dear Child*, page 117; *Collected Works*, Volume 49, page 166.

is stony and they can't afford in prisons to lay out flowerbeds. You must write again.

Kisses to both of you.

Bapu

Gandhi to Mrs. Menon, April 13, 1932[358]

Y.C.P.
April 13, 1932

My dear child,

I am always glad when I hear from you. Your letter is interesting and revealing. You are still fretting somewhat. That you should get over. If we have trust in God, we should not worry even as we would not when we have a trustworthy doorkeeper or guard. And who can be a better doorkeeper or guard than God the never-failing. It is not enough that we sing about such things or have a mere intellectual grasp. It is necessary to feel the thing within. Feeling is exactly like feeling pain or pleasure. It admits of or needs no argument. Who can argue us out of our experience? I write this because I want you to be absolutely free from all care and anxiety.

The idea of giving the children dolls of different races was very good. What is the name of the Hindi girl and what is her province?

Did I tell you that Mahadev was with me?

Kisses to the children.

Love.

Bapu

358. *My Dear Child,* pages 89-90; *Collected Works,* Volume 49, page 305.

Gandhi to Mrs. Menon, May 22, 1932[359]

Y.M.[360]
May 22, 1932

My dear child,

I understand all you are doing. Only you must not work yourself into anxiety. If we simply make ourselves instruments of His will, we should never have [an] anxious moment.

Yes, there is no calm without a storm, there is no peace without strife. Strife is inherent in peace. We should not know it without [strife]. Life is a perpetual struggle against strife whether within or without. Hence the necessity of realising peace in the midst of strife.

It has been hot in Poona this time. As a rule it is never so hot in Poona. But the rains are now coming in and we are having beautiful sunsets and sweet songs of the birds.

Have you been to that patient[361] again?

I told you Mahadev was with me. He spins and cards about five hours daily. He is now spinning very fine counts. Owing to weakness of my hands I cannot do much. I hope you are keeping well.

Love from us all and kisses to the children.

Bapu

359. *My Dear Child*, page 90; *Collected Works*, Volume 49, page 467.
360. Gandhi often referred to the prison as Yeravda *Mandir* (temple).
361. The invalid girl, Nellie Ball.

Gandhi to Nan and Tangai Menon, May 22, 1932[362]

May 22, 1932

Dear Nan and Tangai,

You have sent me a sweet letter.

I see you are making friends with birds. We have made friends with a cat and her kittens. I call her sister. It is delightful to watch her love for her young ones. She teaches them all sorts of things by simply doing them.

God bless you.

With kisses,

Bapu

Gandhi to Mrs. Menon, May 29, 1932[363]

Y.C.P.
May 29, 1932

My dear child,

This is silence time.[364] I have your longish letter-none too long for me. I forgot last time to tell you I had received the book you sent me. I shall read it as soon as I can. Every minute is pre-mortgaged. Any new reading or other work that comes my way has therefore to await its turn unless it is of such paramount importance as to warrant suspension of current work.

Feeling is of the heart. It may easily lead us astray unless we would keep the heart pure. It is like keeping house and everything in it clean. The heart is the source from which knowledge of God springs. If the source is contaminated, every

362. *My Dear Child*, page 117; *Collected Works*, Volume 49, page 468.

363. *My Dear Child*, page 91; *Collected Works*, Volume 49, pages 490-91.

364. Gandhi used to observe silence on Mondays.

other remedy is useless. And if its purity is assured nothing else is needed.

This is written with the right hand, for the left has become worse than the right. There is nothing to worry about.

Only, it must have complete rest. I therefore spin on a wheel which has a pedal and draw the thread with the right hand.

We are three-all well.

Love from us all. Kisses to the children.

Bapu

Gandhi to Mrs. Menon, July 18, 1932[365]

[Gandhi received a long letter from Mrs. Menon on July 18, 1932, in which she said what a fine thing it would be if she could trust God as much as her daughters trusted her. "The kittens surround us every morning, ask for milk and make great noise if they do not get it. This scene is for me a constant reminder that we must trust in God".[366]]

Y.C.P.
July 18, 1932

My dear child,

I have your letter. Do not fret, if you don't hear from me at the expected moment. My correspondence has been upset a bit. I am hoping that the matter will be soon put right.[367] However, a prisoner has got to be satisfied with facilities that may be given to him for the natural satisfaction of his healthy wants.

365. *My Dear Child*, pages 92-93; *Collected Works*, Volume 50, pages 258-59.
366. *The Diary of Mahadev Desai*, Volume 1 (Ahmedabad: Navajivan Publishing House, 1953), page 233.
367. Gandhi's correspondence was being sent to the government and there were long delays before the letters were delivered or before Gandhi was informed that some letters were rejected. He asked for clarification from the government.

When you see the invalid sister, you must tell her I often think of her. I wonder if you ever visit that little school in your neighbourhood for defective children.[368] I thought the institution had earnest workers. If you have the time, I would like you to know more of the institution and its managers and tell me how it progresses.

You tell me how desolate Bajaj's house[369] looked for want of the woman's touch. I have always considered this a result of our false notions of division of work between men and women. Division there must be. But this utter helplessness on the man's part when it comes to keeping a household in good order and woman's helplessness when it comes to be a matter of looking after herself (more here than in the West) are due to erroneous upbringing. Why should man be so lazy as not to keep his house neat, if there is no woman looking after it, or why should a woman feel that she always needs a man protector? This anomaly seems to me to be due to the habit of regarding woman as fit primarily for housekeeping and of thinking that she must live so soft as to feel weak and be always in need of protection. We are trying to create a different atmosphere at the *ashram*. It is difficult work. But it seems to be worth doing.

Remember me and Mahadev to Mrs. Winston when you write to her.

Kisses to the children.

Love.

Bapu

Gandhi to Mrs. Menon, August 4, 1932[370]

[Mrs. Menon, in a letter to Gandhi, asked "why the idea of brotherhood did not take root among nations in spite

368. Gandhi visited that school when he went to England for the Round Table Conference in 1931.
369. Jamnalal Bajaj, a businessman and associate of Gandhi, lived in Wardha.
370. *The Diary of Mahadev Desai*; *Collected Works*, Volume 50, page 328.

of the example set by *Bapu*, Kagawa, Albert Schweitzer and others".[371]]

Y.C.P.
August 4, 1932

Brotherhood is just now only a distant aspiration. To me it is a test of true spirituality. All our prayers, fasting and observances are empty nothings so long as we do not feel a live kinship with all life. But we have not even arrived at that intellectual belief, let alone a heart realisation. We are still selective. A selective brotherhood is a selfish partnership. Brotherhood requires no consideration or response. If it did, we could not love those whom we consider as vile men and women. In the midst of strife and jealousy, it is a most difficult performance. And yet true religion demands nothing less from us. Therefore each one of us has to endeavour to realise this truth for ourselves irrespective of what others do.

Gandhi to Nan and others, August 24, 1932[372]

Yeravda Central Prison,
August 24, 1932

My dear little friends, Nani, Anna, Gillian and Lydia,[373]

I was delighted to have your sweet notes with funny drawings made by you. You do not mind my sending one note for all of you. After all you are all one in mind though not in body. Yes, it is little children like you who will stop all war. This means that you never quarrel with other boys and girls or among yourselves. You can't stop big wars, if you carry on little wars yourselves.

How I wish I was with you to celebrate Nani's and Anna's birthday. May God bless them and bless you all. My kisses to you

371. *The Diary of Mahadev Desai*, Vol. I, page 270.
372. *Collected Works*, Volume 50, page 411.
373. children whom Gandhi had met in Selly Oak when he visited Britain for the Round Table Conference in 1931.

all, if you will let me kiss you and Nani will pass on my love to Esther. Won't she?

Bapu

Gandhi to Mrs. Menon, September 30, 1932[374]

Y.C.P.
September 30, 1932

My dear child,

Even from this distance I could realise your agony. But God never comes to us except through the way of fire. There is a deep unconscious joy felt during such purifying agony. I hope that you were partaker of such joy during the trial. I saw or rather heard your name together with those of Horace Alexander and Andrews among the senders of a loving message from England.[375] I am growing stronger day by day.

You won't expect a long letter from me today. I am expending what energy I have in writing love notes to friends in England.

Love to you. Kisses to children.

Bapu

374. *My Dear Child*, page 93; *Collected Works*, Volume 51, page 157.
375. Gandhi had undertaken a fast in prison on September 30, 1932, when Prime Minister Ramsay Macdonald of Britain announced separate electorates for members of the "untouchable" caste (called *Harijans*, children of God, by Gandhi). The fast was also a penance for the sin of untouchability among Hindus. Indian leaders of varied political persuasions met urgently and agreed on affirmative action to assist the *Harijans* instead of separating them from the Hindu community. Britain accepted the formula and Gandhi ended his fast on the understanding that he would have freedom of correspondence and interviews for *Harijan* work.

Gandhi to Mrs. Menon, October 4, 1932[376]

Yeravda Central Prison,
October 4, 1932

My dear child,

I have your long letter of 4th September. That is a bygone age.

After the fast is like a new birth to me. I am rapidly gathering strength. The lost weight has almost come back. The lost strength will take a little time. The days of agony were also days of inner joy. It was a little penance for the great sin of untouchability committed by millions against their fellow beings. But you know all about it by now.

You must try to get rid of your rheumatism by steam baths and a diet free of much starch and proteins and full of fresh fruit.

I wish you could persuade Nan and Tangai to go to a public school and live down the prejudice, i.e., if the teachers welcome the idea of their going there.

I had a birthday greeting cable from Denmark. The name of the sender was not given.[377]

No more today.

Love from us and kisses to the children.

Bapu

376. *My Dear Child*, page 94; *Collected Works*, Volume 51, page 187.
377. This was apparently a telegram sent by the "Friends of India" society in Denmark.

Gandhi to Mrs. Menon, November 11, 1932[378]

Yeravda Central Prison,
November 11, 1932

My dear child,

I have your latest letter telling me how in ecstasy[379] you would have run to the telegraph office to wire to me and how you subsequently realised that that would have been wrong if only because we are poor people and all the money we had, had to be held in trust for God's service. And I had your long love letter which you had sent to the *ashram* address.

Well, the fast was well worth it even for enabling Menon to give up smoking. The value lies in having given up a thing which had so possessed him. I know that many young men and young women, old men and old women were moved to such restraint and self-denial during the fast week. It shows that it was from God.

I saw and we all admired the group photo with Andrews in it. It was very good. And the bare-bodied Tangai. She looks a perfect picture.

I expect in your next letter to see the account of your visit to the diseased sister.

I had a long letter from the Sunfield School people giving me an account of the new buildings.

You must not trifle with your body by putting into it things that will not suit it. You cannot build your body on pulses. You do not need them at all. Your diet must consist largely of milk, eggs (since you do take them and it is well you do) and whole-meal bread and fruit and green vegetables, salads, tomatoes, spinach, marrow and the like. Even as a soldier keeps his arms clean and in order so must we keep our arms (God-given bodies) clean and in perfect order.

378. *My Dear Child*, pages 95-96; *Collected Works*, Volume 51, pages 399-400.
379. at the news of the termination of the fast by Gandhi.

I have almost regained my strength and am taking normal food. Mira writes regularly every week and is keeping well. Devdas is much better but is overworking himself and so is Pyarelal. Mahadev of course is with me. Tilakam is at the *ashram*. He is a good young man. He is not strong in body.

Enclosed is a letter for the young friend from Denmark.[380] *Ba* is at the *ashram*. I think she has aged more than I have, though she is wonderfully active. Her mind gets easily tired. She worries too much.

Love to you all and in addition kisses to the children.

Bapu

Gandhi to Mrs. Menon, November 25, 1932[381]

Yeravda Central Prison,
November 25, 1932

My dear child,

You are not to worry over the approaching second fast. It may not come at all. But if it does come, let it be a matter of joy to you. Life to be true must be a continuing sacrifice. Enjoyment does not come after. Sacrifice is the enjoyment. All taking must be for greater giving. This is becoming more and more clear to me. Therefore you will watch in utter calmness, joy and prayer what is happening and may happen.

I must not give you more time. Untouchability work leaves no time for love-letters.

Love to you all and kisses to the children.

Bapu

380. This is not available.
381. *My Dear Child*, pages 96-97; *Collected Works*, Volume 52, page 60.

Gandhi to Mrs. Menon, January 5, 1933[382]

Yeravda Central Prison,
January 5, 1933

My dear child,

If I am to cope with my correspondence, side by side with untouchability work, I can only dictate letters for the most part, and even then be brief. It is a fortunate thing that I have been allowed the facility. The untouchability work was going beyond my capacity in spite of the assistance I received from Vallabhbhai and Mahadev. I wish I could do justice to your long love letter. I cannot send you anything like it. I see that you have Andrews settling down in Woodbrooke. You will, therefore, have him always by your side, a strong support to lean on whenever you are in need.

Yes, I have seen the beautiful poem of Shelley's that you have copied for me. I hope you are keeping quite well, and I pray that the New Year has opened for you with much greater inner joy and peace than you have ever possessed.

I was glad for the letter from the ailing sister. Here is my reply to her.[383] Though she has given me her address, as I cannot quite make out her name I send it through you.

Love from us both and kisses to the children to whom a separate postcard is going.

Mahadev sent a book for Tangai and Nannie for Christmas gift. I hope they got it.

Bapu

382. *My Dear Child*, pages 97-98; *Collected Works*, Volume 52, page 369.
383. Text in *Collected Works*, Volume 52, page 368.

Gandhi to Mrs. Menon, February 10, 1933[384]

Yeravda Central Prison,

February 10, 1933

My dear child,

Yes. You did keep me without a letter this time for some weeks and I was wondering why. I must not give you a long letter this time, because the new weekly *Harijan*[385] absorbs me to the exclusion of everything else. You will see the copy that will reach you at the same time as this.

I can quite understand what a source of pleasure Charlie Andrews's presence must be to you and the children.[386] His presence in your midst takes away from me too a load of anxiety on your behalf.

Love from us all to you all.

Bapu

Gandhi to Mrs. Menon, February 17, 1933[387]

Yeravda Central Prison,
February 17, 1933

My dear child,

Nowadays my time is more than fully occupied. Two clear days have to be given to *Harijan* to the exclusion of every other work. Therefore brief as they were, my love-letters have to be

384. *My Dear Child*, page 98; *Collected Works*, Volume 53, page 256.
385. Gandhi started a weekly newspaper, *Harijan*, to promote service to the *Harijans*.
386. C.F. Andrews stayed at the Woodbrooke College for some time under a Quaker fellowship.
387. *My Dear Child*, page 99; *Collected Works*, Volume 53, page 322.

briefer still. But there is some compensation in that you have my general letter in the form of *Harijan*.

I know quite well what my visit to London meant to you.[388] We do not know God's hidden ways. If we only submit to Him, He makes us do many things even unconsciously to ourselves. It will be such a joy to me if you never find yourself in the Valley of Despair, for, to be there even for one moment means lack of faith in a living God.

I enclose herewith a letter for John Hoyland.[389]

Mahadev was delighted to have Tangai's sweet letter.

Love.

Bapu

Gandhi to Tangai Menon, February 23, 1933[390]

Yeravda Central Prison,
February 23, 1933

My dear Tangai,

You have sent me a note not written by you. Therefore you cannot complain if I sent you a reply not written by me.[391]

I know that Uncle Charlie[392] eats much salt, but you must not copy bad habits of elderly people, and eating much salt is a bad habit, and much salt spoils the original flavour of things with which it is mixed.

388. Gandhi was in London from September 12 to December 5, 1931, to attend the Second Round Table Conference on constitutional reform in India as the sole representative of the Indian National Congress. He visited Birmingham and saw the Menons.
389. This letter is not available. Prof. Hoyland of Quaker College, Woodbrooke, had taught in India for 16 years and was a friend of Gandhi.
390. *My Dear Child*, page 119; *Collected Works*, Volume 53, page 380.
391. This was a typed letter.
392. C.F. Andrews.

Uncle Charlie has also a habit of spoiling little children by giving them too many sweets. Therefore, if I were you, I should distribute sweets amongst lots of poorer children and I should feel happy at the thought of sharing with them gifts received from friends.

Love and kisses from us both.

Bapu

Gandhi to Mrs. Menon, February 23, 1933[393]

February 23, 1933

My dear child,

Having dictated this letter,[394] it has got to go to Tangai, though it is going to cost 2½ annas to the Harijan cause. Let us hope that both Nan and Tangai will make up for the loss a thousandfold and more.

Love.

Bapu

Gandhi to Mrs. Menon, March 2, 1933[395]

Yeravda Central Prison,
March 2,1933

My dear child,

I have your letter. I am sending it to Maria.[396] I know she will be delighted with it. Probably you wrote the same time that you wrote to me. Even so, the news of your joining her early will not be stale to her.

393. *My Dear Child,* page 119; *Collected Works*, Volume 53, page 381.
394. Letter to Tangai Menon, above.
395. *My Dear Child,* pages 99-100; *Collected Works*, Volume 53, page 440.
396. Miss Anne Marie Petersen.

I posted a letter last week to Tangai and just gave you a line only. I hope she felt duly proud to receive a letter all to herself, put in an envelope bearing her address, and I hope that she sent me a thousand kisses when she got that letter.

As I am pouring out my heart through *Harijan*, I feel that I have nothing more to say to the members of the growing family.

With all the experience gained in a big hospital, Menon should return as a distinguished specialist in surgery.

Love from us all and kisses to children.

Bapu

Gandhi to Mrs. Menon, March 24, 1933[397]

Yeravda Central Prison,
March 24, 1933

My dear child,

I have your long letter after some waiting. The account of your meeting is very interesting. It was impossible that with all the earnestness and force you could put into your words you could fail to be effective.

The Cross undoubtedly makes a universal appeal the moment you give it a universal meaning in place of the narrow one that is often heard at ordinary meetings. But then, as you put it, you have to have the eyes of the soul with which to contemplate it.

I am glad you are mothering the Muslim girl from Hyderabad. You must tell me more of her when you have known her more.

I never knew that people out there [in England] ever carried loads on their heads. Is what you saw the usual practice in your part of England? What could be the weight, and what are the

397. SN20697; *Collected Works*, Volume 54, page 178.

receptacles made of in which the load is carried ? What is the distance that is covered? Is it the ordinary house-refuse that they contain ?

I hope Hans[398] has found an answer to his prayer.

Maria wrote to me the other day and I saw how glad she was that you were at last coming. She is weary with fatigue, both in body and mind. She is almost on the verge of breaking, and I am anxious that, whilst she is still fit, she should run away to Kashmir and give her body and mind rest for a few months. She needs it desperately.[399]

Love from us all and kisses to the children.

Bapu

Mrs. Menon to Gandhi, April 25, 1933[400]

"Broomhill"
West Malvern
April 25, 1933

My dearest *Bapuji*!

Here I am sitting overlooking from my window the distant hills of Wales. Clouds and sunshine take their turns adding light and shadow to the beautiful many coloured green trees and pastures in the landscape.

I am here for a week's or even a longer stay because I've been ill.

A lady friend of mine, a rich Quaker has sent me here for a change.

398. A German boy living with the Menons at Selly Oak..
399. Please see letter to Miss Anne Marie Petersen, March 21, 1933, below.
400. SN19042 .

My doctor, a lady, states I've run down-why that's a long story-my rheumatism due to bad teeth-which all have to come out, when I've picked up after this attack of malaria, influenza and so on.

But this is quite enough about my complaint, owing to my own or my forefathers' misbehaviour. One can't very easily escape from one's inheritance, that is my experience.

I was more than happy when I received your last letter.

I shall tell you what I know about the dust-bin men here. I have spoken with one of them.

They are generally tall, well built men. They carry their load in ordinary junk-tubs just like a big bathtub weighting about 14 lb.

They have on their head a funny, grey, flat hat, so they easily can place the tub on the head.

The distance they carry their load is only from the backyard to the road and its content is ordinary refuse rubbish and during the winter a lot of ashes and cinders.

The man with whom I spoke told me, it is a very heavy work and the corporation is very difficult to satisfy, but they get a good salary, guineas 30, per week, and they have short hours of work.

The name of my little Mohammedan girl is Mumtaz, I am very fond of her. She is so sweet and charming and clever as well.

Her father is a very influential man in Hyderabad.

She is now going to another college to study domestic science. I shall miss her but I wish many Indian girls would study that subject.

We are trying to persuade C.F.[401] to come to Denmark and give some lectures about India in August. I don't know yet if he can be set free from any other more important work to come, but I know people in Denmark would benefit immensely by getting to know a personality like his in our bewildering time.

401. C. F. Andrews.

Light and shadows fall constantly on our earthy lives, and as I face this beautiful landscape with all light and darkness mixed or blended together in harmony, I understand better that so too it is mixed in our lives-both together.

We get all of us a fair proportion of each, and yet I can't help thinking that some get too much shadow cast on their lives and too few people care to go out of their own easy ways to make other people happy.

I wish, I can train Nani and Tangai always to serve in the great cause of suffering and needy humanity in some way or other.

Nani is inspite of her young age very thoughtful of the need of others in all daily little things.

I cannot hide from you *Bapuji*, that I am anxious regarding the effect the extreme hot climate in S. I.[402] will have upon my two dearest little companions during my many years of loneliness in so many ways.

How could I bear to see them fade away by getting malaria or this or that tropical disease? They are so very strong and healthy now.

A mother's love is both selfish and unselfish, but I believe I would rather suffer anything myself than see them suffer.

They have given me nothing but joy and comfort. Nani-sensitive little soul understands everything, as was she already a little woman, and Tangai strong in will-and passionate in love for her "Mimi" exclaimed the other evening, "Why shall I say 'our Father, who are in heaven', I will say 'our mother who are in heaven'-because a mother is ever so much more than a father and I love you ever so much more than 'Far'"

402. South India.

This exclamation of hers simply shows how necessary both a father and mother are in the bringing up of the children.

She has seen so little of her father, he comes only as a visitor into her life. We must know in order to love; that's, I suppose, why Christ had to reveal us God's true nature and so the more we know him, the more we love him, but the opposite is also true, only as we love him we get to know him intimately as a child knows its father and mother.

I am reading "*The Suffragette Women's Movement*" by E. Pankhurst and I deeply admire the fire and heroic deeds of these champions for women's freedom–there is much similarity between this movement and the one now going on in India; I dare not say more on these lines.

I felt proud by reading that she thinks Denmark to be one of the happiest and most progressive countries in the world.

I am here daily conversing with a noble old lady-but a Tory, she does not understand you in many things-but she believes yet you are one of the builders of the new world to come.

I wish I could write with my left hand, since my right arm and hand has given me pain and so funny without any strength when I write, but you will forgive me this poor scribbling.

How I wish the government would put you on some hill station in the hot season, yet I know, you would never ever accept any privilege before all the nearby fellow sufferers in the jails.

With much love to all of you

your old child

Poor Anne-Maria surely she needs a rest.

Gandhi to Mrs. Menon, May 7, 1933[403]

Yeravda Central Prison,
May 7, 1933

My dear child,

I know what you are passing through. I look upon the coming fast as the richest gift God has yet blessed me with.[404] I must not write more. You should know that it is well whatever the result.

Love for you both and kisses for the children.

Bapu

Gandhi to Mrs. Menon, December 15, 1933[405]

December 15, 1933

My dear child,

I had your touching letter. Well, you have to rejoice in your suffering both mental and physical. You must now do what satisfies your own inner voice. And the end will be all right. Of course Maria will be cut up. But we are all in God's hands, not a blade moves but by His command. If we had all our own ways, the world will go to pieces. It is perhaps as well that our wishes are often frustrated. It is the test of our loyalty to God that we believe in Him even when He refuses to fulfill our wishes. I want you therefore to enjoy perfect peace even while things seem to you to be all going wrong.

403. *My Dear Child*, page 101; *Collected Works*, Volume 55, pages 137-38.
404. Gandhi undertook a week's fast from May 8, 1933, for "self-purification", stressing the need for purity among workers serving *Harijans*. The government released him from prison on that day.
405. *My Dear Child*, page 102; *Collected Works*, Volume 56, page 340.

My prayer, my thoughts and my love are with you. For the rest weekly *Harijan* is my weekly letter to you as to many friends and companions.

Bapu

Gandhi to Nan and Tangai Menon, January 15, 1934[406]

January 15, 1934

Dear Nan and Tangai,

Love and kisses to you. I hope the climate is suiting you and that you are both happy. Are you picking up Malayali tongue?[407] You would write to me frequently.

Love.

Bapu

[Gandhi wrote to C.F. Andrews on February 1, 1934: "You have balanced all the bad news you have given me by telling me that Esther's difficulties are all solved and that Menon has at last decided to come to India. I am sure it is a sound decision, if it is a firm one".[408]]

Gandhi to Mrs. Menon, February 20, 1934[409]

February 20, 1934

My dear child,

I hope Tangai is completely out of fever now. After all you could not get honey at Pondicherry. A basket of fruit with honey

406. *My Dear Child, page 120; Collected Works*, Volume 56, page 492.
407. Malayalam was the language of their father.
408. *Collected Works*, Volume 57, page 78.
409. *My Dear Child,* page 102; *Collected Works*, Volume 57, page 188.

was sent yesterday. Miss Lester[410] is with me now. Agatha Harrison[411] leaves on March 2nd.

Love to you all.

Bapu

Shri Esther Menon

Anne Maria School

Porto Novo

Gandhi to Mrs. Menon, February 22, 1934[412]

February 22, 1934

My dear child,

Two baskets were sent to you. The first one contained honey and Tamil-Hindi books I got on the way. The books might be of use there.

I hope Tangai is now quite restored.

Maria has a grievance against you. I have asked her to talk about it to you freely.

I have read the certificates. They are good. You will tell me of the result of Menon's effort.

Kisses to the children and love to you all.

Bapu

410. Miss Muriel Lester, founder of Kingsley Hall, a settlement in East End of London, where Gandhi stayed during his visit to London in 1931.
411. A British Quaker and friend of Gandhi.
412. *My Dear Child*, page 103; *Collected Works*, Volume 57, page 195

[Gandhi wrote to his wife from Mysore on February 22, 1934: "Esther Menon has returned from England. She came and saw me..."[413]]

Gandhi to Mrs. Menon, February 25, 1934[414]

February 25, 1934

My dear child,

I have your letter. I am glad fruit reached you safe. Another basket was sent. Do not hesitate to ask for more when you have the need.

I don't wonder at Maria's dragging my name with your alleged breach of promise. My conscience is clear. I would not have tolerated your remaining with me if a breach of promise to the children had been involved. But from Maria's letter I gather that her complaint against me is deeper and wider. I wish she would discuss the whole thing with you. And if she does not, you need not worry. I have written to her at length and invited her to unburden herself completely.

Yes, I would like Menon to get the Bangalore job. I have gone through the certificates. They are good and should procure Menon a good job. Do you want the certificates back?

I leave for Patna on 9th March from Hyderabad (Deccan).

Love. *Bapu*

413. *Collected Works*, Volume 57, page 196.
414. *My Dear Child*, page 103; *Collected Works*, Page 215.

Gandhi to Nan Menon, February 25, 1934[415]

February 25, 1934

My dear Nan,

I have your very good letter. I am glad you are spinning every day. You know the golden rule: whatever you do, do well and with your whole heart in it.

Love and kisses.

Bapu

Gandhi to Tangai Menon, February 25, 1934[416]

February 25, 1934

My dear Tangai,

I hope you are quite well. Never wander in the hot sun. Eat plenty of fruit and avoid starchy things.

Love and kisses.

Bapu

Gandhi to Mrs. Menon, [March 15, 1934][417]

[March 15, 1934]

My dear child,

I have your two letters. I am writing this at 12.15 a.m. in Motihari[418] thinking it was 3 a.m. I got up and found it was 12

415. *My Dear Child,* page 120; *Collected Works,* Volume 57, page 215.
416. *My Dear Child,* page 120; *Collected Works,* Volume 57, page 216.
417. *My Dear Child,* page 104; *Collected Works,* Volume 57, page 277.
418. Gandhi spent much time in Bihar between March and May 1934 to promote earthquake relief in the province.

midnight. But I had no desire to sleep with the correspondence in front of me.

I see what you say about Menon. I must not write to the Diwan[419] of Mysore in a personal matter. Menon should apply to all the possible hospitals and go where he may be wanted irrespective of climate. You will have to be where the climate and other considerations suit you and the children for the time being. Like the legal profession, the medical is crowded at the top. Anyway you must keep me informed of what is happening. You should tell Menon that he is at liberty to write to me whenever he likes.

I hope the children are faring well. Yes, you will have to take them to a hill-station during the hot weather.

I understand what you say about the promise. Whether there was a breach or not you alone can judge. I am sorry that Maria was angry over my not going to Porto Novo. She gave me to understand that she had caught the spirit of my self-denial. It was as much a deprivation to me as it was to her. But self-denial to be true has to bring joy not sorrow, never anger.

Love to you all.

Bapu

Gandhi to Mrs. Menon, April 1, 1934[420]

As at Patna,
3.45 a.m. April 1, 1934

My dear child,

I had your long letter after keeping me waiting for a long time. There is not in your letter enough search for truth, that is,

419. Chief Minister, Sir Mirza Ismail.
420. *My Dear Child*, pages 104-05; *Collected Works*, Volume 57, pages 344-45.

the hidden purpose of God. When we know that God Himself is the mystery of mysteries, why should anything that He does perplex us? If He acted as we would have Him do or if He acted exactly like us, we would not be His creatures and He our Creator. The impenetrable darkness that surrounds us is not a curse but a blessing. He has given us power to see the steps in front of us and it would be enough if Heavenly Light reveals that step to us. We can then sing with Newman, "One step enough for me". And we may be sure from our past experience that the next step will always be in view. In other words, the impenetrable darkness is nothing so impenetrable as we may imagine. But it seems impenetrable when in our impatience we want to look beyond that one step. And since God is love, we can say definitely that even the physical catastrophes that He sends now and then must be a blessing in disguise and they can be so only to those who regard them as a warning for introspection and self-purification.

I understand what you say about the children. I am glad that you are in Kodaikanal with the children. You will let me know when Menon gets something. Agatha Harrison is with me. It is rather a trying time for her, not being used to the Indian life. But she is standing it bravely because she wants to learn everything that she can in the shortest time possible. Muriel Lester, I left at Patna. She was not doing well. I return to Patna on the 4th April to leave it on the 7th for Assam. I return again to Bihar about the 25th, pass about a week and then go to Orissa, once more returning to Bihar. You will continue to use the Wardha address.

Love to you and kisses to the children to whom I may not write today.

Bapu

Mrs. Esther Menon

Bourne End

Kodaikanal

Gandhi to Mrs. Menon, June 30, 1934[421]

June 30, 1934

My dear child,

Though I often get up at 2 a.m., I do not overtake my correspondence. There is just time to send you a card of love on your birthday. I know I owe the box spinning-wheel to the children. My love and kisses to them. Mira felt the impulse all of a sudden and went.

Love.

Bapu

Shri Esther Menon

Bourne End

Kodaikanal

S. India

Gandhi to Mrs. Menon, September 6, 1934[422]

September 6, 1934

My dear child,

I held up your letter all these days in the hope of being able to send the answer myself. But I must deny myself that pleasure and dictate this letter if I am to overtake the arrears.

If proof were needed God is proving for me His greatness and goodness every day. You renem-ber the hymn "Count your many blessings". I think it is in Moody and Sankey's Hymn Book. I can't even count the blessings, they are so many. For even the so-called sorrows and pains He sends descend like blessings. If we knew His love, we should know that He has nothing but blessings-and never curses—for His creation.

421. *My Dear Child*, page 106; *Collected Works*, Volume 58, page 127.
422. *My Dear Child*, pages 106-07; *Collected Works*, Volume 58, pages 413-14.

I hope Tangai is quite free and both the children are flourishing. You must have now received the spinning-wheel. I hope that Menon is well-settled.

I am flourishing.[423] My weight has gone up from 94 to 101 lb. I am going through a fair amount of work and taking regular exercise.

Mira is doing good work in London. She expects to be back in October. Andrews was here for over a week and he has now gone to Simla. He will come once more to Wardha before sailing, most probably on the 6th October, for London. He was looking quite well. He has brought a Welsh blacksmith with him from South Africa. Mr. Jones, that is his name, has recently joined the Oxford movement and considers himself a changed man. We all liked him very much. When Andrews goes to England, he will go back to South Africa.

Pyarelal and Mahadev are here. *Ba* has gone with Ramdas to Sabarmati where Ramdas is to have rest and cure for his ailment. Devdas was here for a few days. He left yesterday for Bombay. He is likely to come back for the Working Committee meeting on the 8th. This, you will admit, is a fair family budget of news.

You must write more regularly than you have hitherto done. I don't expect to move from Wardha yet for some time.[424]

With love to you all,

Bapu

Mrs. Esther Menon

Tanjore[425]

423. Gandhi had undertaken a fast from 7 to 14 August as a "penance for intolerance" when a member of the *Harijan* uplift movement attacked an opponent with a club.
424. Gandhi left the *ashram* at Sabarmati after his release from prison and moved to an *ashram* at Wardha in central India before settling at Segaon (Sevagram) near Wardha.
425. Dr. Menon found employment in the government hospital in Tanjore (now "Thanjavur").

Gandhi to Mrs. Menon, September 23, 1934[426]

September 23, 1934

My dear child,

I have your letter and now letters from children. I am glad that they like the place. Of course you cannot give another name to your bungalow, and the expression "Vision Bungalow" is quite good and significant.

Andrews was here a week ago and he would be back on Tuesday from Santiniketan. Mira expects to be in Bombay just in time for the Congress session.

Ramdas had fever and general debility. He is now better.

I understand that the spinning-wheel was sent to Porto Novo, and I hope that it has now come to you. I would like to know the progress made upon it.

How nice it would be to have you here at this time![427] The weather is superb-very cold, not too much sunshine and yet enough of it.

With love to you all and kisses to children,

Bapu

Mrs. Esther Menon

Vision Bungalow

Tanjore

426. *My Dear Child*, pages 107-08; *Collected Works*, Volume 59, page 71.
427. Gandhi was in Wardha.

Gandhi to Mrs. Menon, October 14, 1934[428]

October 14, 1934

I have your two letters before me. You are having a very bad time. But I hope that Nan is getting better. I can understand her longing for Denmark. This is surely a difficult task.

It is often a dilemma as to which is the best course to adopt. It is a constant spiritual struggle in which, with the godfearing, right triumphs over wrong.

When Maria comes there, give her my love.

Ramdas is better. He is still in a hospital in Ahmedabad. *Ba* is with him.

Mrs. Esther Menon

Vision Bungalow, Tanjore

Mrs. Menon to Gandhi, [before November 14, 1934] (Extracts)[429]

[The following letter by Mrs. Menon concerning Gandhi's campaign to open all Hindu temples to *Harijans* (members of the so-called "untouchable" caste) appeared in a Danish periodical in 1934. The following is a re-translation of the letter from Danish.[430]]

Dear, beloved *Bapuji*!

Since my return to India, I have given much consideration to the question about admitting untouchables to the temples. From a religious and social point of view it is quite all right that we

428. Pyarelal Papers; *Collected Works*, Volume 59, page 173.
429. *Porto Novo*, Copenhagen, 1934, No. 9, pages 208-211.
430. Please see letters from Gandhi to Mrs. Menon on November 14, 1934, and January 5, 1935.

want the untouchables to have the same rights and privileges as the caste Hindus. But as I have approached this question from a quite different angle, I have asked myself: why not teach the pariahs-or whatever it is we call them-something higher and better? God does not live in temples created by human hands, nor does He take the shape of images created by us.

"Blessed are the pure in soul, for theirs is the Kingdom of Heaven", Christ said.

"The hour cometh when ye shall worship neither in this mountain nor that-but God is a spirit: and they that worship him must worship him in spirit and in truth". In Tanjore, you see many temples–small and large, some very filthy and dirty and decayed. Do we find the living God there? Where there is love, there is God-God could live in the cottage of the poorest pariah if he has opened his heart.-What do the temples mean for the modern Hindu at the present? Little or nothing at all. The temples have significance only for the proud, orthodox Brahmins, who are ready to burst in pride over the caste they are born into–without any merit of their own–while they shut out their brothers from the rights they would like to enjoy. And on top of that, they have the audacity to have the religion accept this breach of truth, love and justice. It takes a lot of impudence to call any human "untouchable"–whether the reason is birth, occupation, or anything else. Really, the Brahmins have made God so petty and biased, just like the Jews did in the ancient times, when millions groaned and lamented under their heavy yoke. In his own country, Jesus refused to recognise such a restrictive, partial God, and he had to fight against all the strange misconceptions the Pharisees and the scribes had about God. If He came to India in our time, He would act in the same manner. He would have to take up the struggle against the Brahmins and others; he would face the same situation as he did when he overthrew the moneylenders and the merchants selling from the temple. Indeed he would say: "My house shall be called the house of prayer: but ye have made it a den of thieves. I do not want burnt offerings of fatted calves, goats, or oxen, nor coconut, flower, or incense sacrifices. I only want love and a humble heart". If I were a pariah in modern day India, I would not care the least about being admitted to the temples, because inside me a voice would say: "God is not in temples. He dwells in my heart when I can forget myself. He is in my humble home. He is where innocent children play. He is in the workshops and in the great, wonderful nature. He is with the poor and the suffering". And of course as a Christian, I see God best and most clearly when I look into the face of Jesus Christ.

Do not think that I do not see the many wrongs and defects and misunderstandings within the Christian church when I meet them–regardless of appearance–first and foremost within myself. I try to fight them, but the one basic truth remains that God is love and loves all his children, even though we contradict that with our different ways of life. But there is no use in "putting new wine into old bottles, or putting a piece of new cloth unto an old garment".

Look at Russia: because the church as an institution denied the common man his rights, millions had to rid themselves of the church's yoke, it only gave stones for bread.-*Bapuji*! You know how much you have meant to me for nearly twenty years, and what you still mean to me. I have not returned to India to quarrel over religious questions, but to share, to receive, and to give. However, if I am not true to myself, I cannot be true to you, who put the truth over anything else. Therefore, I had to write this letter to you in all humbleness, and after careful consideration, but without consulting anything else than my own conscience. I know that I do not have your ability to give for sacrifice or service, or your genuine love towards India's poor. I know that you consider me as one of your many children who struggle for more light, love, and truth–not only into our own lives, but also into the whole world. Therefore you will also give me your opinion of this matter, and correct me where you think I am mistaken.

Love,

Your child

Gandhi to Mrs. Menon, November 14, 1934[431]

November 14, 1934

My dear child,

I have your letter. I am glad Nan is restored and no more wants to go to Denmark. Of course, there is no place for any child better than the mother's lap. But that is an ideal state which we may all strive after, though we may ever fail to reach it.

I am sorry to hear about Maria. Who can replace her in her school except you? And just now you are out of the question. I wish a way out was found to enable her to go to Denmark and get the change she so badly needs.

I do not remember having received your letter on the Temple-entry Bill.[432] Was it sent after my returning to Wardha? If you can reproduce the argument please do so and I shall endeavour to reply.

I did hear about the death of Jack Hoyland's son. Andrews was then here. We sent a joint cable of condolence, and I had a full account of the death from Hoyland. It was a sad thing.

Mira returns on the 22nd bringing with her Khan Saheb's daughter[433] who was having her education in London. Mary Barr[434] is here from her village home and has brought a friend just arrived from England. Mary has taken wonderfully to the *ashram* life. The weather here just now is superb. Ramdas returned with *Ba* four or five days ago. He is very weak, but I think he will pick up

431. *My Dear Child,* pages 108-09; *Collected Works,* Volume 59, pages 339-40.
432. A bill concerning the opening of Hindu temples to *Harijans* was introduced in the Central Legislative Assembly in 1934, but was later withdrawn by the sponsor.
433. Dr. Khan Saheb was a leader of the Indian National Congress in the North-West Frontier Province.
434. Miss F. Mary Barr, who taught at a Mission school in India, became a follower of Gandhi and stayed in the *ashram* several times. She spent many years in village upliftment work. She went to South Africa in the 1940s and served a term of imprisonment in 1946 during the Indian passive resistance against racial discrimination.

strength here. Andrews is likely to be here in December, for a fortnight or so. How is Menon doing?

Love to you all.

Bapu

Mrs. Esther Menon

Tanjore

Gandhi to Mrs. Menon, January 5, 1935[435]

Delhi,
January 5, 1935

My dear child,

If this letter can intensify the wishes, then this is to reciprocate your wishes. It is freezingly cold here. The 4 o'clock prayer bell has gone.

Of course, *Harijans* need ever so much more than mere temple-entry for their spiritual satisfaction.[436] Temple-entry is not so much their spiritual need, as its grant is that of the arrogant caste Hindus. They can have no spiritual grace so long as they deny to their fellows in faith the same right of worship that they claim for themselves. Is not this quite clear?

With love and kisses added for the children,

Yours,
Bapu

[PS]

In Delhi till 20th at least, 28th at the most. Then Wardha.

435. *My Dear Child,* page 109; *Collected Works,* Volume 60, pages 57-58.

436. *Harijans* (members of the "untouchable" caste), though Hindu, were excluded from many Hindu temples. Gandhi and his followers opposed the exclusion and resorted to passive resistance to open the temples to *Harijans.*

Gandhi to Mrs. Menon, January 17, 1935[437]

January 17, 1935

My dear child,

I have your letter and the children's. Tangai is a wise girl and so she has learnt to resign herself to the sorrows that come to her.[438] The spirit of resignation is bad when sorrows come out of our conscious errors; but when they come for reasons we do not know and cannot know, resignation is the proper thing. In other words, constant endeavour and surrender to the will of God have to go hand in hand.

Your description of your visit to Porto Novo and Maria's losing herself in her work is very good.

My feet won't let me walk, because immediately I try, the crack reopens.

C. F. Andrews could not write to you as he had no time whatsoever. It was touch-and-go whether he would be able to catch the steamer he did.

Both A.I.S.A.[439] and A.I.V.I.A.[440] are absolutely non-political associations.

You must come to Wardha some day. Delhi is too far for you. What is Menon being paid for hospital work? We leave here, at

437. My *Dear Child*, page 110; *Collected Works*, Volume 60, pages 87-88.
438. Tangai's health was very delicate at this time, with frequent ailments.
439. All India Spinners' Association.
440. All India Village Industries Association.

the latest, on the 28th instant.[441] We have been passing through a very severe spell of cold weather.

Love.

Bapu

Mrs. Esther Menon

"The Vision"

Tanjore (S. India)

Gandhi to Tangai Menon, January 17, 1935[442]

January 17, 1935

My dear Tangai,

You are a very brave girl cheerfully going through the illness you get from time to time. You must ask Daddy this question: "Why do I get these sores when you are yourself a doctor? You should find a way of helping me". I hope you are much better now.

Love and kisses.

Bapu

Gandhi to Nan Menon, January 17, 1935[443]

January 17, 1935

My dear Nan,

You have written a very good letter in good steady hand. You were quite right in wishing me a Happy [New] Year because you wrote your letter on the 27th December. But there is no use now in my returning the wish, for the New Year is well on its way.

441. Gandhi was in Delhi from December 29, 1934 to January 28, 1935.
442. *My Dear Child*, page 121; *Collected Works*, Volume 60, page 88.
443. *My Dear Child*, page 121; *Collected Works*, Volume 60, page 89.

You must tell me how you felt when you began your spinning on the new wheel. Do you know how to spin on the *takli*[444]?

Love and kisses.

Bapu

Gandhi to Mrs. Menon, February 25, 1935[445]

Wardha,
February 25, 1935

My dear child,

Your letter. Why apologise for the length of your letter? You do not write too often.

Mrs. S.[446] was here for a day. She is a good, well-meaning woman. She told me she was with you.

Yes, the children have to be in Kodai for their health's sake. It grieves me to think that Menon has still to draw funds from Denmark. But of this we must talk when we meet.

So Maria cannot go home! It is no easy work to love India with all one's heart.

Send my love to Nellie Ball when you write to her.

C. F. Andrews is in W. A.[447] He expects to come to India in April.

Mira had a very narrow escape in a motor-car accident. She is all right now.

Bapu

444. a portable contrivance for spinning.
445. *My Dear Child*, page 111; *Collected Works*, Volume 60, pages 261-62.
446. The full name is not legible. It may be Mrs. Saraswati Ambujammal.
447. West Africa.

Gandhi to Mrs. Menon, [after February 25, 1935][448]

[After February 25, 1935]

My dear child,

I have just finished reading your precious letter. My heart was weeping as I was reading it. Do you know this Tamil proverb—"*Thikkatrava-nukku theivamay thunai*"? It means God is the help of the helpless. He will help you and comfort you. You must not lose faith in His mercy and His healing power.

You should have written to me much earlier than you have done. But better late than never.

You should tell Menon all that the children feel. What is done is done. God had a purpose behind this marriage. You are neither spent nor bent.

Your way is clear. You should take the children to Denmark or England if your expenses can be easily found. If you cannot stand that climate, you should return to India leaving the children to the care of those who would take them.

If this is not possible, you should live on a hill where you can be all the year round and bring them up as Indians in Indian surroundings. I think they are too good to resist this. To bring them up in India in a European school is fatal for their moral growth.

Of course I should love to have you and the children by my side. But they won't stand the climate and probably the surroundings also. Do not hesitate to write to me as often as you need. I am well enough to attend to your letters.

I tried to secure something good for Menon but failed, i.e., I could not secure the salary he would need. But if he is freed of the care of the children and even you, he can take up an ill paid post but one in which he will have ample experience.

448. *Collected Works*, Volume 60, pages 264-65.

Whatever the ultimate issue, you must not be anxious about anything. Remember that God takes the burden of all our cares on His broad shoulders if we will but let Him. This is as true as it is true that I am writing to you. Only His way is not our way, His shoulders are not like ours. But there is all the beauty in doing His will.

Love.

Bapu

[Gandhi wrote to C.F. Andrews on July 29, 1935: "Esther's is a tough problem. My opinion is that Menon should stick to India but not to Tanjore. Real skill has its price everywhere".[449]]

Gandhi to Mrs. Menon, [On or after April 30, 1936][450]

[On or after April 30, 1936]

My dear child,

I have your long letter. I have read it with the deepest interest. You have a tough problem in front of you. If you can, you should come to Nandi Hill to see me. I reach there on 10th May.[451] God will guide you. You must not worry. Take things as they come to you when you cannot alter them.

I am writing this from the village Segaon[452] where I want to settle down. Mirabai is here already. She will go to some other village, if I settle down here. I do not want any of the old co-workers with me, if I can help it.

Love.

Bapu

449. *Collected Works,* Volume 61, page 295.
450. *My Dear Child,* page 112; *Collected Works,* Volume 62, page 357.
451. Gandhi arrived in Nandi Hills, near Bangalore, for a month's rest.
452. A village five miles from Wardha where Gandhi set up an *ashram.* He later renamed it Sevagram.

Gandhi to Mrs. Menon, May 14, 1936[453]

[Mrs. Menon moved to Kodaikanal, a hill station, with her two daughters, as they could not bear the hot climate in Tanjore.]

May 14, 1936

My dear child,

May God give you full strength to live up to your motto, "It is no easy matter to count always loss as gain, in joy as well as pain". I know anyway that your life is not in vain. Of course you are right in not coming to me. You will come, when God wills it.

I hope Tangai is quite well again. Kisses to the children. See if they would write to me. Here is a little note for them.

Don't coax them to write.

Love.

Bapu

Gandhi to Nan and Tangai Menon, May 14, 1936[454]

Nandi Hill,
May 14, 1936

Dear children,

Do you remember that there was a time when you used to write to me? Should you not-now that you have grown in years

453. *My Dear Child*, page 114; *Collected Works*, Volume 62, page 398.
454. *My Dear Child*, page 122; *Collected Works*, Volume 62, page 399.

and wisdom? I was sorry to hear of Tangai's illness. The hat for delicate children like you is a necessary article of wear.

Love and kisses from

Bapu

[PS.]

Esther will tell you all about where I am at present.

Gandhi to Mrs. Menon, May 18, 1936[455]

May 18, 1936

My dear child,

You are being tested. Why should you have 'flu even in a cool place like Kodai? But I know you will keep your peace even in the midst of tortures and live up to your motto. You will tell me when you are free. My prayers and my love are with you.

Bapu

[Gandhi wrote on May 25, 1936, to Mrs. Saraswati Ambujammal to see Esther Menon on his behalf and befriend her, if possible. He wrote to her again on June 6: "I am glad you went to Esther. If you found her glad to receive your visit, I would like you to go to her as often as you conveniently can".[456]]

Gandhi to Mrs. Menon, [June] 19, 1936[457]

[June] 19, 1936

My dear child,

You are naughty. You will write on all the sides of your letter without giving any direction as to where you began writing in all

455. *My Dear Child*, page 114; *Collected Works*, Volume 62, page 416.
456. *Collected Works*, Volume 62, page 445 and Volume 63, page 21.
457. *My Dear Child*, page 113; *Collected Works*, Volume 63, pages 71-72.

the margins. Why don't you add one more sheet? But no more of grumbling. I sent Saraswati and Kanti as I thought you would like to see them.

Strange! I have a letter from Maria this week. She shows considerable anxiety about you.

It must be torture to K.[458] that he cannot do just what he thinks is best for want of funds. We have however to take comfort from the fact, God does not always allow us to do what we think is the best. I suppose we don't always know what is best.

Do not make the children write to me. Let them write when they are led to do so of their own free will.

I hope you have completely recovered from your illness. How I should love to see you as hale and hearty as you were when we first met. You were such a picture of health that I had thought you to be incapable of getting ill.

Love.

Bapu

Gandhi to Nan, June 26, 1936[459]

Segaon,
June 26, 1936

My dear Nan,
I had hoped to send you a long chatty letter but I never got the time. Now Esther sends me a reminder. So here is this note to tell you that though I cannot write, I can never forget you. I hope both of you are happier than before.

Love and kisses to both of you.

Bapu

458. Presumably Kuhni, her husband.
459. *My Dear Child*, page 122; *Collected Works*, Volume 63, page 99.

Gandhi to Mrs. Menon, March 26, 1940[460]

Wardha,
March 26, 1940

My dear child,

It seems ages when I heard from you last. Therefore it gave me joy to see your letter to Charlie who has forwarded it to me for disposal. Why have you not been writing to me? I know you are careful about my time. But I do want an occasional line from you.

The girls are the biggest problem for you. But there too you have to trust God to lead you. No use fretting about things we cannot mend.

How are you keeping yourself?

Charlie had a narrow escape.[461] He is still bed-ridden but out of danger. I saw him often enough when I was in Calcutta. Mahadev, who has just returned from Calcutta, brings news of slow but steady progress.

For the family here, I am keeping fit, *Ba* has a persistent cough and is weak, Mahadev is living here. The place is fairly crowded. Mary[462] is still in the village of her choice sticking to it in spite of difficulties.

M.[463] writes to me now and then.

Love.

Bapu

460. *My Dear Child*, page 115; *Collected Works*, Volume 71, page 373.
461. Gandhi had visited C.F. Andrews, who had an operation in March, at the hospital in Calcutta.
462. Miss F. Mary Barr.
463. Probably Anne Marie Petersen.

Letter to Mrs. Menon, [after March 26, 1940][464]

Wardha,
[After March 26, 1940]

My dear child,

You must trust God and be cheerful. Everything pales before the tragedy that is taking place in Europe. Can nothing be done for Tangai ?

Love.

Bapu

464. *My Dear Child*, page 116; *Collected Works*, Volume 71, page 374.

MISS ANNE MARIE PETERSEN (1878-1951)

Biographical Note

Miss Petersen was born in Rosilde near Svendborg, Denmark on September 1, 1878. After working for some time as a teacher, she decided to become a missionary. She had studied at a free school and a folk high school and was greatly influenced by Niels Frederik Severin Grundtvig (1783-1872), Danish philosopher and educator. He had founded the movement for folk high schools, "schools for life" which combined academic education with study of current affairs and training in agriculture. He stressed that the gospel should be taught in the mother tongue, with respect for the culture of the individual's community. He declared: "First a man, then a Christian". His liberal views on religion gave rise to a church movement, the Grundtvigians, as one of the constituents of the Lutheran Church in Denmark.

Miss Petersen arrived in India at the end of 1909, sent by the Grundtvigian group in the Danish Missionary Society (DMS) as assistant to Edvard Loventhal at his mission in Vellore, but was later transferred to the DMS in Madras so that she could work among women. She studied Tamil and became a teacher in a girls' school, but was not satisfied with working in the existing DMS schools.

She had a great desire to establish a national school for girls in accordance with the views of Grundtvig. She felt strongly that students in missionary schools should not be forced to adopt the Western way of life and become alienated from their people. She believed that the church must become Indian, based on Indian culture, in order to influence the nation to accept Christianity. She felt that her identification with the culture and aspirations of the people, including the struggle for national indepen-dence, would contribute to this process of acceptance of Christ. She was against racism and supported full equality between Europeans and Indians in the missions.

In 1916, she obtained authorisation from the DMS to visit a number of schools around India to enable her to prepare plans for a girls' school. She chose Miss Esther Faering, a younger missionary, to accompany her.

During the course of the tour, they stayed at Gandhi's *ashram* in Ahmedabad for three days in January 1917 to observe the small school there. They found that Gandhi's views on education were in harmony with those of Grundtvig. They were also greatly impressed by Gandhi and the life at his *ashram*. Gandhi too developed fondness for them. They began to correspond with Gandhi and identify with the movements led by him for social reform and the freedom of India.

In her report to the Danish Missionary Conference in February 1917, Miss Petersen said that the teaching of students in English created alienation and learning problems, as well as contempt for Indian culture. She preferred national schools teaching in the language of the people with emphasis on the history and culture of India. She proposed a national Christian girls' school, with a balance between academic and practical subjects, in accordance with the views of Grundtvig. The Board of the DMS authorised her to establish a school along the lines of her proposal, and to obtain funding from Grundtvigians. She left for Denmark and was able to secure assurances of financial support.

Two weeks before she returned to India in 1919, Miss Faering had resigned from the DMS as it disapproved her correspondence with Gandhi and her engagement with a non-Christian. Miss Petersen stood by Miss Faering, invited her for Christmas and began to correspond with Gandhi.

She too resigned from the DMS in January 1920, when the Society rejected a proposal for equality between Danish and Indian missionaries.

Gandhi was at that time leading a nonviolent non-cooperation movement for India's freedom in which tens of thousands of volunteer's courted imprisonment. He combined political action with a constructive programme including the use of *Khadi* (handspun and hand-woven cloth) as a means to provide employment and alleviate poverty, abstention from alcohol and social reform (especially rejection of untouchability practised by the Hindus). Miss Petersen (Sister Maria, for Gandhi) began to spin, wear *Khadi* and use Indian products as much as possible. She became a strong supporter of the Indian movement for freedom.

Gandhi's respect for Christianity, the inspiration he derived from the Sermon on the Mount, his espousal of reform of Hinduism and his emphasis on love and non-violence in the struggle for national freedom appealed to her as a Christian. She felt that participation of Christians in the freedom movement was essential to pave the way for Christianity in India, while support of the alien government would alienate the Indian people.

After meeting Gandhi at a public meeting he addressed in Vellore on August 14, 1920, she wrote to him that the meeting had "more or less decided my future".

"I have thrown myself at the feet of India. At the same time I know that in Christ alone is my abode and I have no longing and no desire but to live Him, my crucified Saviour, and reveal Him for those with whom I come in contact. I just cling to His feet and pray with tears that I may not disgrace Him as we Christians have been doing by our behaviour in India... If we who bear His name were true to Him, we would never bow ourselves before the Powers of this world, but we would always be on the side of the poor, the suffering and the oppressed. But we are not, and therefore I feel myself under obligation not only to Christ but to India for His sake at this time of momentous importance for her future".

She was especially attracted by Gandhi's call to boycott government schools and establish national schools. She wrote to Gandhi:

"Only by indigenous education can India be truly uplifted. Why this appeals so much to me is perhaps because I belong to the part of the Danish people who started their own independent, indigenous national schools. The Danish Free Schools and Folk High Schools ... were started against the opposition and persecution of the State. The organisers won and thus have regenerated the nation".

Gandhi published her letter in his paper, *Young India*, especially to show that his movement was not anti-Christian or anti-European. He wrote to Miss Faering on September 2, 1920: "Anne Marie... (and) I have fallen in love with each other".

In November 1921 when the government asked the missionaries to sign an undertaking pledging loyalty, she signed with a declaration that as a Christian she would collaborate with everything good and promote loyalty to God and not to kingdoms of the world. The authorities blacklisted her and excluded her school from government grants. She was made subject to restrictions under the Foreigners' Registration Act.

On September 17, 1921, she founded *Seva Mandir* (Temple of Service) and a school for girls, the National Christian Girls' School, at Porto Novo (Parangipettai), south of Madras, in what is now Chidambaram district. Teachers and children lived in the school as in an *ashram*. Spinning was introduced in the school from the beginning.

Gandhi laid the foundation stone for the school at a large public meeting and stayed that night at Petersen's.[465]

While Miss Petersen had a broad vision, the school was a small institution for many years as it received no government grant and the contributions from Denmark were modest. It had only 13 pupils in 1924. But while other national schools established under the inspiration of Gandhi did not survive, her school continued in existence because of her faith and determination.

Meanwhile, in the support group in Denmark, there was criticism of her identification with the Indian freedom movement, and opposition to her views on an independent Indian church with its own rituals. During her visit to Denmark in 1926-27, the support group dissolved itself, charging that the mission run by Miss Petersen in India "is more part of the Indian national movement than it is a Christian piece of mission work".

She was able to secure the formation of a new support group that agreed to give missionaries the right to freedom in their work, but there was a drop in contributions from Denmark, while the needs of the mission increased.

Miss Petersen arranged for Esther Faering (now Mrs. Menon) to travel to Denmark for health reasons and supported further medical studies of Dr. Menon in Britain. That cost a vast amount of money, and the mission faced serious economic difficulties. The number of students in the *ashram* went down to six. But Miss Petersen did not lose hope, and continued to support Gandhi and the Indian national movement.

465. The school was in her home until a building was built. It was formally opened and a Dedication Ceremony held in January 1924; Gandhi could not attend as he was in prison.

When Gandhi launched the Civil Disobedience movement in 1930, she offered her services, and gave refuge to families of volunteers who went to prison. She attended a rally inaugurating the movement in south India and said Christian prayers.

When Gandhi returned to India in January 1932 after the Round Table Conference in London, she went to Bombay to welcome him and had a private conversation with him.[466]

Later when Gandhi went on a fast for self-purification on the issue of untouchability, she issued a moving appeal to the people of India to remove the sin of untouchability.

She visited Denmark from 1935 to 1937. Popular governments were established in Indian provinces in 1937 and the British authorities granted her a visa at the request of Rajaji, the Chief Minister of Madras.

Miss Petersen was active in Gandhi's programmes for village industries and for basic education. In October 1937 when Gandhi presented his "Wardha scheme of education" for rural India, she offered to adopt the curriculum.

But, again, during the war, she faced difficulties as the Congress government in Madras resigned and Denmark was under Nazi occupation. Gandhi sent her a small grant to show his support.[467]

466. Miss Petersen met Gandhi on several occasions after the first meeting in January 1917. She visited him in hospital in Poona in February 1924 when he fell ill while a prisoner. She saw him before leaving for Denmark in 1926, and at the Congress session in Madras in December 1927. She met him in Bombay when he returned from London in January 1932, and in prison in April 1933. She visited Gandhi's *ashram* at Sevagram later in the year. She met him again at a national educational conference at the *ashram* in January 1945 and at a constructive workers' conference in Madras soon after. And in January 1946, she met Gandhi at the 60th session of the Indian National Congress.

467. After Gandhi was assassinated in 1948, Miss Petersen wrote in the Porto Novo Mission newsletter:
"Without Gandhi I would never have become as Indian as I became. What a significance he had on me and on our mission.... When

After Indian independence in August 1947, the Madras provincial government gave her right of residence without the restrictions of the Foreigners Registration Act. The authorities recognised the school and provided grants. They helped the school to expand and to open a Teachers' Training Institute.

Miss Petersen–lovingly known as *Periamma* (great mother) died on January 9, 1951.

After her death, a trust with two Danish and four Indian members, and an Indian principal ran the school. By 2000, it had more than 2,000 pupils and 60 teachers.[468]

Twelve letters from Gandhi to Miss Petersen and two from his secretaries, published in the *Collected Works of Mahatma Gandhi*, are reproduced below, along with one additional letter by Gandhi and ten letters by Miss Petersen to Gandhi.[469]

For further information, please see:

Bent Smidt Hansen, *Dependency and Identity: Problems of cultural encounter as a consequence of the Danish mission in South India between the two world wars.* Quebec: World Heritage Press, 1998.

Tine Elisabeth Larsen, *Anne Marie Petersen, A Danish Woman in South India–A Missionary Story 1909-1951.* Chennai: Lutheran Heritage Archives, 2000.

Denmark was raped by Germany, he wrote to me: 'I am sorry for Denmark and for you. Tell me, what I can do to help you'. And it was not empty words. As you know he helped..." [33]

468. Tine Elizabeth Larsen, *Anne Marie Petersen, A Danish Woman in South India*, page 213.
469. Five other letters from Gandhi to Miss Petersen, between 1934 and 1944, were reported to be at *Seva Mandir*. (Bent Smidt Hansen, *Dependency and Identity*, page 291). We have been unable to obtain copies of these letters.

Correspondence with Gandhi

Miss Petersen to Gandhi, December 1, 1919[470]

38 Broadway
Madras
December 1, 1919[471]

Dear *Bapuji,*

Excuse me for not writing for such a long time. I have been roaming about here and there and have no time as yet and so I find it very difficult to write. However I have been following you in your touring and your work and am with you in thought and prayer. I am longing very much to see you, so please do inform me if you are coming to Madras. There is some talk about it, I hear, and I am sure we need you very earnestly here. Probably I shall still leave Madras tonight and as soon as I get a house, I shall write a long letter to you. Thanks for the money (Rs. 150) which I here return. I also owe something for cloth. Please ask the officer to send me my bill and I will pay it off. I find it very difficult to get real *swadesi* cloth in Madras or these parts of India and I am going to use only Indian things as far as possible hereafter.

With my kind regards to Mrs. Gandhi, Devadas and all other friends in the *ashram* and with you. Mrs. Bittmann sends her kind regards.

Yours

Anne Marie

470. SN19816. This letter, during Gandhi's leadership of a mass movement for freedom, reflects her defiance of the restrictions imposed by the British rulers on foreign missionaries in India.
471. Miss Larsen suggests that this letter was probably written after September 1, 1920. Tine Elizabeth Larsen, *Anne Marie Petersen,* page 74.

Gandhi to Miss Petersen, January 13, 1920[472]

Dear Miss Petersen,

I was delighted to hear from you after a long absence. As soon as I heard that you wanted Miss Faering to join you during Xmas, I had no hesitation in saying that she should respond to your wish. I can thoroughly appreciate the Christian sentiment that friends and relations should gather together and have sweet communion during the Xmas season. I must confess to you that Miss Faering's presence in the *ashram* is uplifting for us all. She is such a good-natured loving girl with all the loftiest aspirations that anyone can be capable of. We are looking forward to meeting her again. I only wish that she will be able to keep her health here and become a better and a stronger Christian for her presence in the *ashram*. As I have so often told her, her living at the *ashram* can be justified only if she not only retains undiminished her Christianity but that, in the environment of the *ashram*, it becomes purer and more ref[ined] than ever before. I consider myself a Hindu of Hindus. I believe that I have a fine perception of the truth of Hinduism and the priceless lesson I have learnt from it is that I should not wish that others may become Hindus but that they become best specimens in their own faith. I hold an unfortified day cast in your lot with me here. Let not the Indian summer frighten you. I can easily arrange for you to pass the two hottest months of the year in a cool place. There are many such in India. They are not inaccessible.

Miss Petersen to Gandhi, [before September 8, 1920][473]

[Miss Petersen met Gandhi at a meeting addressed by him in Vellore in August 1920 and wrote him a long letter which Gandhi published in *Young India*,

472. *Collected Works*, Volume 16, page 477 .
473. *Young India*, September 8, 1920.

September 8, 1920, under the title "A Missionary on Non-Cooperation". He introduced the letter as follows:

"I commend to the attention of the readers of *Young India* the thoughtful letter received from Miss Anne Marie Petersen. Miss Petersen is a lady who has been in India for some years and has closely followed Indian affairs. She is about to sever her connection with her Mission for the purpose of giving herself to education that is truly national.

"I have not given the letter in full. I have omitted all personal references. But her argument has been left entirely untouched. The letter was not meant to be printed. It was written just after my Vellore speech.[474] But it being intrinsically important, I asked the writer for her permission, which she gladly gave, for printing it.

"I publish it all the more gladly in that it enables me to show that the movement of non-co-operation is neither anti-Christian nor anti-English nor anti-European. It is a struggle between religion and irreligion, powers of light and powers of darkness..."]

Dear Mr. Gandhi,

I cannot thank you enough for your kindness and the way in which you received me and I feel that meeting more or less decided my future. I have thrown myself at the feet of India. At the same time I know that in Christ alone is my abode and I have no longing and no desire but to live Him, my crucified Saviour, and reveal Him for those with whom I come in contact. I just cling to His feet and pray with tears that I may not disgrace Him as we Christians have been doing by our behaviour in India. We go on crucifying Christ while we long to proclaim the Power of His resurrection by which He has conquered untruth and unrighteousness. If we who bear His name were true to Him, we would never bow ourselves before the Powers of this world, but we would always be on the side of the poor, the suffering and the oppressed. But we are not,

474. Gandhi spoke at Vellore, a town south of Madras, on August 14, 1920.

and therefore I feel myself under obligation not only to Christ but to India for His sake at this time of momentous importance for her future.

Truly it matters little what I, a lonely and insignificant person, may say or do. What is my protest against common current the race to which I belong is taking and (what grieves me more), which the missionary societies seem to follow? Even if a respectable number protested it would not be of any use. Yet were I alone against the whole world, I must follow my conscience and my God.

I therefore cannot but smile when I see people saying you should have awaited the decision of the National Congress before starting the non-cooperation movement.[475] You have a message for the country, and the Congress is the voice of the nation-its servant and not its master. A majority has no right simply because it is a majority.

But we must try to win the majority. And it is easy to see that now the Congress is going to be with you. Would it have done so if you had kept quiet and not lent your voice to the feelings of the people? Would the Congress have known its mind? I think not.

I myself was in much doubt before I heard you. But you convinced me. Not that I can feel much on the question of the *Khilafat*. I cannot. I can see what service you are doing to India, if you can prevent the Mahomedans from using the sword in order to take revenge and get their rights. I can see that if you unite the Hindus and the Mahomedans, it will be a master stroke. How I wish the Christian would also come forward and unite with you for the sake of their country and the honour not only of their Motherland but of Christ. I may not feel much for Turkey, but I

475. Gandhi launched the nonviolent non-cooperation movement in August 1920 in protest against brutal repression in the Punjab and in defence of Turkey and the Caliphate (*Khilafat*), thereby uniting Hindus and Muslims in a common struggle. The Indian National Congress endorsed the movement shortly *after* it was launched.

feel for India, and I can see she (India) has no other way to protest against being trampled down and crushed than non-cooperation.

I also want you to know that many in Denmark and all over the world, yes, I am sure every true Christian, will feel with and be in sympathy with India in the struggle which is now going on. God forbid that in the struggle between might and right, truth and untruth, the spirit and the flesh, there should be a division of races. There is not. The same struggle is going on all over the world. What does it matter then that we are a few! God is on our side.

Brute force often seems to get the upper hand but righteousness always has and always shall conquer, be it even through much suffering, and what may even appear to be a defect. Christ conquered, when the world crucified Him. Blessed are the meek; they shall inherit the earth.

When I read your speech given at Madras[476] it struck me that it should be printed as a pamphlet in English, Tamil, Hindustani and all the most used languages and then spread to every nook and corner of India.

The non-cooperation movement once started must be worked so as to become successful. If it is not, I dread to think of the consequences. But you cannot expect it to win in a day or two. It must take time and you will not despair if you do not reach your goal in a hurry. For those who have faith there is no haste.

Now for the withdrawal of the children and students from Government schools,[477] I think it is a most important step. Taking the Government help (even if it be your money they pay you back), we must submit to its scheme, its rules and regulation. India and

476. Speech on Non-cooperation, delivered at a public meeting in Madras beach on August 12, 1920. *Collected Works*, Volume 18, pages 143-54.

477. The non-cooperation movement involved boycott of government schools and the establishment of national schools. In the national schools, instruction was in the mother tongue. Apart from academic subjects, the students were taught Hindi (the national language), agriculture, spinning and weaving.

we who love her have come to the conclusion that the education the foreign Government has given you is not healthy for India and can certainly never make for her real growth. This movement would lead to a spontaneous rise of national schools. Let them be a few but let them spring up through self-sacrifice. Only by indigenous education can India be truly uplifted. Why this appeals so much to me is perhaps because I belong to the part of the Danish people who started their own independent, indigenous national schools. The Danish Free Schools and Folk-High-Schools, of which you may have heard, were started against the opposition and persecution of the State. The organisers won and thus have regenerated the nation.

With my truly heart-felt thanks and prayers for you,

[As noted earlier, Miss Petersen founded a national girls' school in Porto Novo in 1921. It was named *Seva Mandir*–temple of service.]

Miss Petersen to Gandhi, January 29, 1924[478]

[Gandhi fell ill in prison and was taken to hospital in Poona.]

Seva Mandir
Porto Novo
January 29, 1924

My beloved *Bapu*,

I shall not tire you by writing a long letter to you. I would have written and would have run to you at once if it had not been for this very reason.[479] For is it not selfishness the very craving of one's heart wanting to see you? You know I am sure that in my prayer and my thoughts I am always with you. I also thought it

478. SN 8186.
479. Gandhi, then a prisoner in Yeravda Central Prison, Poona, was recuperating at Sassoon Hospital after an operation for appendicitis.

would be better to wait and see you later--but I am now afraid that they will take you from us again and if it is [not] only a botheration for you if my visit could in any way a love offering to you I shall come to Poona.

I am glad however that Kuhni[480] has seen you and that Esther has started with her little girl today. They will be there about the time you get this letter. Give them your blessing and it is enough for me. In God's own good time I also will be allowed to meet you again.

May God strengthen you day by day and help us all to fight the good fight and win the prize.

Your loving

Maria

My love to *Ba*. I also send my school program to *Tambi*[481] Devadas. He will tell you if he finds it worth reading for you--or keeping till a better time.

Miss Petersen to Devadas Gandhi, January 29, 1924[482]

Seva Mandir
Porto Novo
January 29, 1924

My dear friend,

I have written a letter to *Bapu*. Hope he may be allowed to read it.[483] I am also sending you my school program. Keep it and read it for *Bapu* when he is able to hear it or a bit of it.

480. Mr. Kuhni (or Kunhi) Menon, husband of Esther Faering.
481. brother in Tamil.
482. SN8187.
483. Gandhi was still a prisoner. He was released unconditionally on 5 February.

I should love to come and see him if there is danger as I fear and as your letter to Esther also made us understand that there is doubt about his release. I have therefore wired to you to ask whether I can be allowed to come and see *Bapu*. I do not like to worry him and tire him whom we love and would spare for ... and worry if possible. You will know best whether it would be best to come or to stay away.

My best wishes and prayers

Sister Anne Marie Petersen

Miss Petersen to Gandhi, September 23, 1924[484]

My beloved *Bapujee,*

I send you this as a token of my love and prayer.[485] Not that I have not spun more in all these days. I have. I am trying to do my duty. But this cotton is Devacotton,[486] cannot be used by man and therefore it is for you. It was grown in my garden. I plucked it early in the morning when the white soft little cotton children were wet with dew, tears shed from above for our sake. I took the offering, spun it from the seed so that no machine should crush and soil it. I have prayed when I span it and I am now weeping over it for my heart is faint with fear for you and India.

Accept it as my love offer. May God strengthen you and accept your sacrificing yourself.[487]

Maria

484. SN10199.
485. Miss Petersen sent yarn spun by her.
486. Deva means God.
487. On September 17, 1924, following riots between Hindus and Muslims, Gandhi commenced a 21-day fast as "penance and prayer".

Miss Petersen to Gandhi, September 24, 1924[488]

Seva Mandir, Porto Novo
September 24, 1924

My beloved *Bapujee*,

Do not be afraid. I do not write to trouble you or to persuade you to give up your fast. What right have I even to ask you to live for love's sake?

I had to wire for the little children, and I am sure all the children of India join in begging you to give up your fast and live for their sake. What have they done, poor innocent little ones, that this curse should fall on them? For if you die there is no future for India as a people. Therefore *Bapu* I beg with tears do not sacrifice your life except you are sure there is no hope for India. We who love you and are doing what we can and have suffered (sometimes I thought beyond endurance) for India, cannot and will not go on working for a lost cause. Ten times then better die! Continue your fast and prayer till India repents and allows God to create in her a new heart. And if she does not, she is not worthy to live. And we who have a life hidden in God, need not worry for our own sake.

But this I beg of you, if you have still hope for India, suffer to live for her sake.

Give up your fast when the doctor tells you that your strength is failing you.

God does not test us beyond endurance. We have all sinned by failing to do as much as we ought to do and for our sake you suffer. But say when we ask forgiveness and promise to live a new life: "Father, forgive them, for they know not what they do".

God strengthen you and us all and be with us in life or death.

Maria

488. SN10199-A.

Gandhi to Miss Petersen (telegram), March 5, 1925[489]

MISS PETERSEN

PORTO NOVO

REACHING MADRAS SATURDAY MORNING "EN ROUTE" VYKOM.[490]

GANDHI

Miss Petersen to Gandhi, June 7, 1926[491]

Varlose, Denmark
June 7, 1926

My dear *Bapujee,*

Rumours are kept up that you are coming to Helsingfors.[492] Is it true or not? Then you promised me to come also to Denmark and stay here for some time. Please let me know for sure whether we can expect you or not. I do not know whether it will be good or not for you and for us for you to go here so I will not ask you. There are many things here which you will dislike and disapprove of. And yet Denmark is a sweet and in many ways a good little country. If it be *the will of God do come* and it will surely be for the best both for us and for India. But you have promised to let me arrange, and to let me know as soon as possible. I am busily engaged in meetings myself and it will be difficult for me to come to Finland with you, but in Denmark you must put yourself in my humble and gentle hands so that I can try to protect you against being torn by newspapermen and other rascals. I shall get up the very

489. *Collected Works*, Volume 26, page 231.
490. Gandhi visited Vykom, in Travancore State, where a *satyagraha* (non-violent resistance) was being carried on for some time against the denial of the use of a public road to members of the "untouchable" caste, in order to promote public opinion against this evil practice of "untouchability".
491. SN10764.
492. Gandhi was invited to the World YMCA Conference in Helsingfors and considered attending it.

best men to form a committee to receive you and arrange a few meetings (many or few as you like) and show you the Folk High Schools and farms and whatever you would like to see.

For one thing I am sure it would help you to be stronger to go for such a little trip. I am ever so much stronger myself–and better I hope as I promised you to be. It is good for me to be in my old house for some time. And yet I am longing back to India so very badly and remain here only for the sake of India.

How are all the friends in the *ashram*? Please give my love to *Ba* and to Miss Lester and all friends!

All love
Maria

My permanent address is
Ferritslev
Ullerslev
Denmark

A wire could be sent to
Annemarie
Ferritslev
Ullerslev

Or if they do not know Ullerslev in India (it is a telegraphic station though) write Nyborg and it will be sent to me.

A.M.

Miss Petersen to Gandhi, May 4, 1928[493]

"Gopal Lodge"
Kodaikanal
May 4, 1928

Dear *Bapujee*,
I am so sorry for you that you have lost your comrade and co-worker Maganlal K. Gandhi.[494] It is a great loss not only for you

493. SN14647.
494. A nephew of Gandhi and manager of the *ashram*.

and the *ashram* but for the country when a selfless, silent worker as he was leaves us and that before we have reached the goal of *Swaraj*. He died bravely on the battlefield, and may we not take comfort in the belief that he is called to a higher service! God must know and He cannot dispense with any faithful servant. More eagerly than we can do must the all loving God and Father work for the final goal; His kingdom on earth as in heaven, which we dimly see and strive towards "Except the wheat dies it cannot bear fruit" and so let us believe that all those who give their life for India in selfless sacrifice are seeds sprouting for its harvest.

God help and strengthen you and his wife and children... Dear *Bapu*, do not think I am writing for the sake of formality and do not think I am forgetting you and all friends in the *ashram* when I am not writing. You know and can see from my writing how difficult it is for me to express myself in a foreign tongue.

But my heart is with you always and especially in hours of sorrow and trial. I know what sorrow and separation from our dearest ones is, but also I know where to find comfort.

And *Bapu* I have for a long time wanted to write to you and ask you to spare yourself as much as possible till and for our final struggle. Without you we will not succeed.

I wish it was possible to start boycott of foreign cloth. If we could carry one practical thing like that through it would mean so much, give us strength and confidence. I shall be the first to sign a pledge not to use foreign cloth-say for four or five years and get many to sign it. It must be made simple and clear, and it must not be something complicated and difficult. But perhaps Bardoli must see its fight through first.

We are doing our little bit of work. For the first time we are getting on with spinning and have started one loom for our own *khaddar*. The girls are not spinning much yet-there are only a few but they spin fine and good yarn from 20 to 40 counts which we must have for saris here in the South.

Give my love to *Ba* and convey my sympathy to Maganlal's wife and children.

Yours loving

I have come up here for the hot weather. I could not bear the heat down in the plains.

Gandhi to Miss Petersen, May 11, 1928[495]

The *Ashram*,
Sabarmati,
May 11, 1928

My dear Petersen,

I was glad to have your letter. I know that if you did not write it is not for want of affection but it is because of affection. I have you often in my thoughts.

Yes, Maganlal's death is a heavy blow, if I am to consider this to be a Godless universe and we a purposeless creation; but when I realise that the hand of God is in everything, the grief itself turns to joy and gives me zest for greater service, greater dedication.

Yours sincerely,

Miss Marie Petersen

Kodaikanal

Miss Petersen to Gandhi, January 15, 1929[496]

National Christian Girls' School
Porto Novo,
January 15, 1929

My dear *Bapujee*,

It is indeed a long time since I have written to you. As I told you, it is only wasting your time and energy writing to you when I have nothing particularly to write about. But I am following

495. SN13222; Collected *Works*, Volume 36, page 307.
496. SN15140.

closely in all that is going on, rejoicing with you and India over everything good, every conquest, every step nearing the goal. Bardoli conquest is a great step towards *Swaraj*.[497]

And now shall I congratulate you in having again been pushed into politics. Anyhow I congratulate India that you [have] been forced to take the actual leadership.[498]

And my reason for now writing to you is to wish you God's blessings in the new year, and the years to come. May God give you strength to do your appointed work and may He help us all to do our share. If we can do nothing else may we be more earnest in our prayers. But *Bapu*, although it may be useless, still I cannot help asking you again and again: Do try to take care of yourself as much as you possibly can, for our sake, for India's sake! I read that you have given up taking milk. That troubles me. Excuse me for saying so, but sometimes it seems to me, you are playing with your life. Your life is too valuable to be experimented on. I shall pray that God will preserve you in spite of your many experiments and vows and principles and that His will may be your only principle. Have you not seen again that India cannot do without you? And what will this year bring us? One year seems so short a

497. In 1928 the government increased the land tax in Bardoli district by more than 20 percent. At Gandhi's suggestion, Vallabhbhai Patel resigned his position as mayor of Ahmedabad and went to Bardoli to lead a no-tax campaign. The government resorted to severe repression, confiscating the land, cattle and crops of the peasants, and arresting hundreds of farmers. After resistance for six months guided by Gandhi, the government released the resisters from prison, returned confiscated property and agreed to hold an inquiry into the justification for the tax increase. Following the enquiry the tax increase was reduced to a little over 5 percent.
The resistance in Bardoli was a sort of dress rehearsal for the nation-wide civil disobedience in 1930.

498. In December 1928, the Indian National Congress decided, in a resolution moved by Gandhi, that if Britain did not grant dominion status for India by the end of 1929, it would define its objective as complete independence and launch civil disobedience. It was understood that Gandhi would lead the movement again. He toured the country in 1929 to rally support for the coming struggle.

time. But it is much better to say: Today, then tomorrow. When I came first to India, somebody told me, the first word in Tamil you will learn is "tomorrow" and there is indeed too much of tomorrow which never comes, because when it comes there is another tomorrow. So I am glad a time limit has been put to get *Swaraj* or to take it. For and with God one year is as thousand. May this year be His year and the world will see what He can do.

I wonder whether two Danish ladies, one Mrs. Hørup and Miss Olsen who came to India to see you have been fortunate enough to get your *darshan*.[499] I know your time is very precious, but it would be a great pity for them to have come all the way in vain. And they are old ladies or shall I say elderly like myself? They love India, but even they have been influenced by Miss Mayo with regard to Indian women.[500] Also they are not believers in God and it may be a real blessing for them to stay in your *ashram* with you for some time.

Has Esther written to you lately? She was very upset when she read in the Danish papers about the changes in the *ashram*. Your own statement the same newspapers may not publish.[501] Anyhow I think she gets *Young India*. I have also written reassuring her of the truth.

499. *Darshan*, a term of reverence used for seeing a deity or a saintly person. Mrs. Ellen Horup and Miss Cathinca Olsen spent a few days in the *ashram* and met Gandhi.
500. Miss Katherine Mayo, an American, wrote *Mother India*, a book, which painted a gruesome picture of the society in India, and the condition of women.
501. Gandhi wrote in *Young India* (November 4, 1928) that all the inmates of the *Satyagraha Ashram* at Sabarmati had not succeeded in observing its rules regarding truth, celibacy, nonviolence etc., interpreted strictly. It was therefore decided to maintain the *ashram* as an ideal, but to run all its external activities (e.g. industries to help poorer classes) in the name of "*Udyog Mandir*". The *ashram* would keep for itself a small ground for prayers.
The managing committee of *Udyog Mandir* decided to stick to the rules of the *ashram* but to treat them as ideals toward the fulfilment of which every member would constantly strive.
An experiment was also being made of running a single kitchen for the entire *ashram*. *Collected Works*, Volume 38, pages 22-24.

Menon is staying in England (Birmingham). He is working very hard, has passed his examinations well and hopes to finish this year, and we may see them back at the end of this year, if Esther is well enough. She has not yet picked up strength. She has been operated for appendicitis. But more than from that I think it is the malaria that has so much pulled her down. She is in Denmark together with her two sweet little girls. I suppose you are not going to Europe this year as things are. When you can go as messenger for a free

India, then only can you feel free to go, perhaps. May it soon come to pass.[502]

My love to *Ba* and all friends in the *ashram*,

Your Maria

Gandhi to Miss Petersen, January 20, 1929[503]

Satyagraha Ashram, Sabarmati,
January 20, 1929

My dear Maria,

I was delighted to receive your letter after such a long absence. It is not at all certain that I have launched on active politics. I do not know what part I have to play during the year. The next month will perhaps decide.

You are needlessly anxious about my dietetic experiment. Believe me that experiment too is under God's guidance as I understand it.

You are quite right about the time-limit. Let us see what is in store for us at the end of the year.

502. Gandhi and the Indian National Congress were at this time discussing whether to attend the round table conference proposed by the British Government to consider the future constitution of India.
503. SN15141; *Collected Works*, Volume 38, page 373.

I am sorry that Esther is not yet quite restored. I knew about the operation for her appendicitis. Menon was expected to do no less than what he has been doing. However, I am glad that he has come up to the expectation.

You have surmised well about the European visit. In 10 days I shall know definitely whether I am to go to Europe or not. But you are quite right. It would be only as a representative of free India that I should go to Europe. But here too God's will be done.

The Danish sisters[504] are here. They have been here for the last 4 or 5 days. They are passing a week here at the *ashram*.

Yours sincerely,

Miss Marie Petersen

National Christian Girls' School

Porto Novo (S. India)

Gandhi to Miss Petersen, August 16, 1931[505]

Ahmedabad,
August 16, 1931

I was delighted to hear from you after a long time.

My collapse[506] had nothing to do with my health. It was purely the welling up of emotion in me that overpowered me for the moment. This has happened to me more than once. I am keeping quite fit and there is no cause for anxiety. Do not stop writing for fear of taking up my time. Only don't expect me always to reply. Had I gone to Europe I should certainly have sought out Esther

504. Mrs. Horup and Miss Olsen.
505. SN17484; *Collected Works*, Volume 47, page 303.
506. While speaking at a meeting of the All India Congress Committee in Bombay on August 8, 1931, Gandhi expressed his anguish at incitement to violence between Hindus and Muslims. He was overwhelmed by emotion and could not proceed with his speech for some time. *Collected Works*, Volume 47, page 273.

and Menon. But God is great and merciful. At the right moment, he lifted the weight off my shoulders.

Miss Petersen

Porto Novo (S. India)

Gandhi to Miss Petersen, January 22, 1932[507]

[The following was re-translated from a Danish text that appeared in *Indiens Venner* (Friends of India), Copenhagen. Gandhi was arrested in January 1932, soon after his return from London; Miss Petersen met him in Bombay before the arrest. Gandhi was in Yeravda Central Prison from January 5, 1932 to May 8, 1933.]

My dear Maria,

Do not fear anything. Often we do not know what is good for us, or for our cause. When we are not driven by pride, but have surrendered ourselves to Him, then whatever happens, will be for the best.

Sardar Vallabhbhai (Patel) is together with me. We are both happy and of good heart.

With love,

Bapu

Write whenever you want and have the opportunity.

Gandhi to Miss Petersen, June 4, 1932[508]

June 4, 1932

"Be careful for nothing" is one of the verses that has ever remained with me and taken possession of me. If God is, why need

507. *Indiens Venner*, Copenhagen, 1932, No. 6, page 2.
508. *The Diary of Mahadev Desai*; *Collected Works*, Volume 50, page 15.

I care? He is the Infallible Caretaker. He is a foolish man who fusses although he is well protected.

[Gandhi wrote to Miss F. Mary Barr on November 30, 1932: "I am glad you are with Maria and your picture of her family which includes our four-footed kinsfolk is instructive and it is just like her. I do not mind her not writing to me. Whilst I welcome her letters when she has anything to say to me, I do not want her to steal a single minute merely for writing to me because somebody else is writing".[509]]

Gandhi to Miss Petersen, March 2, 1933[510]

March 2, 1933

My dear Maria,

I enclose herewith letter from Esther[511] which I have no doubt you will like and prize. We shall all look forward to their coming in autumn and it will be a great relief to me.

Mary Barr wrote to me that she was likely to accompany you during your visit to Kashmir. I hope it is coming off and that it will do you good and give you a little bit of bracing air and rest to your tired limbs and mind.

I hope you are getting your copy of the *Harijan* regularly.

Yours sincerely,

509. *Collected Works*, Volume 52, page 96.
510. SN20431; *Collected Works*, Volume 53, page 443.
511. The letter is not available.

Miss Petersen to Gandhi, March 14, 1933[512]

Seva Mandir, Porto Novo
March 14, 1933

My dear *Bapujee*,

Thank you so much for your two loving letters, the last enclosing Esther's. I am glad they are coming. I do *need* them. I am so tired that I hardly know how [to] go through these last few days and also I am afraid of the journey to Kashmir.

I hope however that the stay there will help me, so that I can come back a new and better being and that with Menon's help we can start some work amongst the poor and needy around us, also do something for the *Harijans*. It is good of you that you will see me on their account.[513] It is more for the sake of what I wish to do, than what I am really doing.

I have not even adopted the little *Harijan* girl I wanted to adopt in your name. None came as sent by God and I have not been able to go about seeking any. Also I am afraid of taking a new child when I am going away and giving all the responsibility to others. It is altogether a great responsibility and very difficult task to bring up children, and give them the right kind of education. What most they need is love–love that knows no bounds. I feel my shortcomings so keenly–especially when I am so tired as now when even their happy noise upsets me. But all visitors who have been here remark that the children are so full of joy and life. That is a comfort for me. And there are a great many children–especially girls who need a home and enough to eat and motherly love–even if they are sometimes too much for me. I will not miss one of those I have and I shall open my home and my heart for as many as I can, when I return from rest. There are so many things I long to talk to you about *Bapu*–mostly educational questions. I wonder

512. SN20596.
513. Gandhi was in prison at that time. He was allowed visitors in connection with his movement for the service of *Harijans* (members of the so-called "untouchable" caste).

whether you or Mahadev Desai[514] ever got the book I sent him for Xmas. It was a book I thought you would be interested in about "Education for Life" (*The Danish Education*, by an Irish woman, Noel Davis).[515] I shall bring it to you when I come.

But in order to be sure that I will be allowed an interview with you, I shall write today and ask the Superintendent[516] permission. It would be too disappointing if I came to Poona and could not see you. Then I would rather go straight to Kashmir via Madras Delhi Frontier route and ask Maria Barr[517] to join me in Delhi. I am glad she is coming with me. She is the sweetest girl and best companion one could think of. All here–teachers, servants, pupils–loved her. I really hope she will become a member of your *ashram* and do some good work there now when *Ba* and Mirabehn are not there.

Don't trouble to answer this letter. If I get a favourable reply from the Superintendent I shall come some day the first week of April.

My very best regards to your companions and love to you.

Maria

Gandhi to Miss Petersen, March 21, 1933[518]

March 21, 1933

My dear Maria,

Just one line to acknowledge your letter and to tell you that generally speaking the Superintendent's permission is not needed for people to visit me on matters of untouchability, because a

514. Secretary to Gandhi.
515. Noelle Davies, *Education for Life*. London: Williams & Norgate Ltd., 1931.
516. Of Yeravda prison, near Poona.
517. Mary Barr, a teacher and social worker from England, who was an admirer and associate of Gandhi.
518. SN20646; *Collected Works*, Volume 54, page 150.

general order has already been passed by the Government. Lest therefore there is any delay in your receiving an official reply, I write this to tell you that you will be admitted if you come during the ordinary hours, which are between 1 p.m. and 4 p.m. except on Sundays, and also on Wednesdays and Thursdays, if you can possibly avoid the last two days. Sundays have to be avoided for the convenience of the administration, Wednesdays and Thursdays for my *Harijan* work.

The sooner you get away and rest your tired body the better for you and your work of love.

Yours sincerely,

[Gandhi wrote to Miss F. Mary Barr on April 26, 1933:

"I am sorry that Maria had such a breakdown. The fact is that she postponed her rest too long. I hope however that she is now benefiting by the relaxation. For it is not so much the bracing air as the relaxation of mind and body that she needs. She must therefore give herself as much rest as she can both to body and mind, and as a quack doctor I suggest to her that she must eat sparingly, restricting herself as much as it is possible to milk and fruit of which there is so much to be had. She may take salad vegetables but she does not need them. If she carries out these very simple instructions to the letter she will find that she will derive the greatest benefit from the change. She must not at present think of writing her book. She may write it when she has completely recovered her vitality and lost the haggard pensive look that she had about her when I met her. I must not omit to add that she ought not to take those two poisons, *ghee*[519] and coffee, so bad for nerves. I suggest a home-made substitute, hot water, Kashmir honey and a few drops of lemon. She will find this to be a complete, effective substitute for milk or coffee or cocoa.

"I suggest a novel recreation for both of you. In going about for your walks, make a search for all the *Harijans* you can find and add to your knowledge of Hindi by trying to make yourselves understood by them and in understanding them. And do not forget

519. melted butter.

the prescription for avoiding cold. Keep yourselves moving as much as possible in the open air".[520]]

[Miss Petersen met Gandhi at his *ashram* around November 1, 1933.]

[Rajkumari Amrit Kaur, who acted as secretary to Gandhi, wrote to Miss Barr on July 6, 1935: "Regarding Maria Petersen's letter *Bapu* wishes me to say that there is no likelihood of his going to Denmark".[521]]

Pyarelal[522] to Miss Petersen, November 26, 1944[523]

Sevagram, "via" Wardha,
November 26, 1944

Dear sister,

Bapu was very glad to have your letter of 3rd inst. He is sorry he cannot write to you himself as he has been forced to further curtail his work owing to overstrain.[524] In fact he has almost reached the limit of his capacity and has had nature's warning signals which he cannot ignore. He does not want to undertake a fast, but he is faced with a moral dilemma and he is praying to God for light. He will not undertake the fast unless he has the clearest indication that it is the will of God.

I hope you had a favourable response from the trustees of the Kasturba Memorial Fund[525] with regard to your proposal about your school.

What you write about *Ba* is but too true.

520. *Collected Works*, Volume 55, page 25.
521. *Collected Works*, Volume 61, page 236.
522. Gandhi's secretary.
523. Pyarelal papers at the Nehru Memorial Museum and Library; *Collected Works*, Volume 94, page 177.
524. Gandhi had been released from prison on May 6 because of illness.
525. Mrs. Kasturba Gandhi died in prison on February 22, 1944. The Kasturba Gandhi National Memorial Fund was set up soon after.

You will certainly come whenever you feel like coming.

Yours sincerely,
Pyarelal

Sister Maria

Seva Mandir

Porto Novo

Gandhi to Miss Petersen, August 23, 1945[526]

Poona,
August 23, 1945

My dear Maria,

Your half angry and half loving letter. Why are you so foolish as to take what a third party says? Kasturba[527] is a wholly non-sectarian organisation. Who was the third party who gave you to understand that only Hindus could apply? The thing has to come before me. It has not yet. If you have applied send me a copy of the application too. You know that Aryanayakum is a Christian. Raihana Tyabji is a trustee. So much for the Trust.

When there is independence, why should you fear the majority? If you have God with you and the majority have not, should you still fear? And if both have God between them who should fear whom? Is there then any question of majority and minority?

Let us pray.

Love. *Bapu*

Miss Maria Petersen

Seva Mandir

Porto Novo (S.I.)

526. Pyarelal papers at the Nehru Memorial Museum and Library; *Collected Works*, Volume 81, page 157.
527. Kasturba Gandhi National Memorial Trust.

Gandhi to Miss Petersen, September 5, 1945[528]

September 5, 1945

My dear Maria,
I have got all your papers now. I see that it is nobody's fault at the Centre. Anyway I am on the track now.

Love.

Miss Maria Petersen

Seva Mandir, Porto Novo,

South India

Gandhi to Miss Petersen, October 2, 1945[529]

October 2, 1945

My dear Maria,
Your letter.

You are foolish, so are we all, some more, some less. Therefore why worry? You must be well and live long enough to see your work flourish.

Your application is under way. The Board meets some time this month when I hope the application will be finally considered. The ideal will be to find your expenses from the surroundings. We must strive to reach it.

Of course you will see me in Madras when I come there. Have you fixed your date for the departure overseas?[530]

528. Pyarelal papers at the Nehru Memorial Museum and Library; *Collected Works*, Volume 81, page 230.
529. Pyarelal papers at the Nehru Memorial Museum; *Collected Works*, Volume 81, page 302.
530. Miss Petersen left for Denmark in June 1946 and returned at the end of 1947.

Send my love to Esther when you write to her and accept it for yourself.

Bapu

Miss Marie Petersen

Seva Mandir

Porto Novo (S. India)

Rajkumari Amrit Kaur[531] *to Miss Petersen, October 6, 1945*[532]

Poona,
October 6, 1945

Dear Miss Petersen,

The enclosed[533] is self-explanatory. *Bapu* wishes me to send it to you and would like a reply by return post as the matter of giving your institution help is coming up for consideration when the Trust Committee meets here on the 16th, 17th and 18th inst.

I imagine there will be no difficulty in your giving an undertaking that if the K.M. Fund helps you with money you will consent to have at least one or two of its representatives on your governing body and that there will be nothing done in the way of conversions in the institution.

Yours sincerely,
Amrit Kaur

Miss Marie Petersen

Seva Mandir

Porto Novo

531. She acted as Gandhi's secretary for some time.
532. Pyarelal papers at the Nehru Memorial Museum and Library; *Collected Works*, Volume 94, page 221.
533. Letter from L.N. Gopalaswamy, Secretary, Tamil Nadu Provincial Committee of the Kasturba Trust, in which he had expressed the inability of the Trust to give financial help to Miss Petersen's *ashram* at Porto Novo.

Gandhi to Miss Petersen, October 16, 1945[534]

Poona
October 16, 1945

Dear Maria,

I have read your letter to Rajkumari. I must say your letter is unsatisfactory. That you are going to Denmark and that during your absence the institution will remain closed should have been sufficient for the withdrawal of the application. Was it good or necessary to bring in the matter of conversion? When you and Esther came to me, it was, I think, common between us that conversion from one faith to another was needless and created heart-burning. One's faith expands by removing the bad in it and absorbing the good and new from the others. You have every right to hold the opposite view. My point is simple. You had a decisive cause for with-drawing your application without raising an irrelevant issue.

I hope you will have a good time in Denmark and will return hale and hearty.

Love.

Bapu

Miss A.M. Petersen

Seva Mandir, Porto Novo

534. Pyarelal papers at the Nehru Memorial Museum and Library; *Collected Works*, Volume 81, page 362.

MRS. ELLEN HØRUP (1871-1953)

Biographical Note

Mrs. Ellen Hørup, journalist, feminist and pacifist, was daughter of Viggo Hørup, an anti-militarist who founded the Copenhagen daily *Politiken*. She became interested in Gandhi in the 1920s while living in Rome. She visited India with Miss

Cathinca Olsen, Danish painter, ceramist and designer, in January 1929. They stayed at Gandhi's *ashram* at Sabarmati for over a week. After return to Denmark Mrs. Hørup wrote articles on Gandhi and his *ashram*.

She was in India again for four months in the winter of 1930-31 with Ms. Caroline (Bokken) Lasson, Norwegian singer, actress and writer. They met Gandhi, as well as other Indian leaders–Jawaharlal Nehru, Maulana Abul Kalam Azad and Subhas Chandra Bose–and visited Anne Marie Petersen's school in Porto Novo. Unlike most foreign tourists, they stayed at Indian homes, visited villages and observed the poverty of the people. Mrs. Hørup published a book about the journey to India, *Gandhis Indien* ("Gandhi's India"), in December 1931. She said about her visits to India: "His (Gandhi's) ideas, my admiration for him, the longing to meet the man who gave me what I have been seeking all my life–something which together is called devotion, reverence and love–was what led me twice to India".

Miss Olsen and she were with Gandhi in London during the Round Table Conference on Indian constitutional reform at the end of 1931.

Mrs. Hørup was active in informing European public about India's struggle for independence and promoting support. She set up *Indiens Venner* (Friends of India Society) in Denmark in October 1930. Miss Anne Marie Petersen, Esther (Faering) Menon, Miss Cathinca Olsen and Mr. and Mrs. Johan Bittmann (former missionaries in India) were among the members of the organisation, which was active for several years. Ms. Lasson set up a Friends of India Society in Norway.

Mrs. Hørup organised an International Conference for India in Geneva on October 6, 1932. An International Committee for India was established with Dr. Edmond Privat of Switzerland as President, Mlle. Madeleine Rolland (sister of Romain Rolland) as Vice-President and Mrs. Hørup as honorary secretary. Mrs. Hørup moved to Geneva. After a second conference on March 23, 1933, mostly for people in Geneva, the Committee organised a third International Conference on September 19, 1933. Delegates attended it from several European countries. The speakers included Bhulabhai Desai and Subhas Chandra Bose, leaders of the Indian

National Congress, and Mrs. Hamid Ali. The Committee published a bulletin, *Indian Press*, until 1935 when it was suspended after the Indian National Congress decided to discontinue publicity abroad.

Throughout the 1930s Mrs. Hørup wrote many articles on Gandhi and the Indian struggle for freedom. She also wrote on international affairs, especially on the rise of fascism and the danger of war, in many newspapers and periodicals, including *Modern Review* and *Calcutta Review* in India.

In the mid-1930s, Mrs. Hørup drifted somewhat from Gandhi. She explained, in a speech to *Indiens Venner* in Copenhagen on November 23, 1936, on "My Relationship with Gandhi", that Gandhi continued to mean to her "the apostle who would bring, not only to India but to the entire world, the gospel of the future–the abolishing of violence from mankind". But India now meant more than Gandhi to her as she learnt of the different movements in India. She then referred to her differences with Gandhi as regards the rights of women, birth control, religion, the caste system, class struggle, industrialisation, trade unions etc., echoing the criticism of Gandhi at that time by Indian radicals.

In 1937 when the Friends of India Society in Norway nominated Gandhi for a Nobel Peace Prize, Mrs. Hørup wrote to a number of influential persons and organisations for support. She received positive replies from Romain Rolland, C.F. Andrews, Bart de Ligt, Maria Montessori, Henrik Pontoppidan (Danish Nobel Laureate), Professor Ludvig Quidde (German Nobel Peace Prize laureate), Hassing Jorgensen and Edv. Larsen (Danish members of Parliament), and numerous other Danish organisations and individuals.

Mrs. Hørup was a founder and a member of the board of the Danish-Indian Friendship Union, established in 1948, after India became independent.

For further information, please see:

Holger Terp "Ellen Hørup and Mohandas Gandhi" in Frede Højgaard (ed.) *Friends of Gandhi: Inter-war Scandinavian Responses to the Mahatma* (NIAS Report No. 7, 1991).

Ellen Hørup, *Gandhis Indien*. Copenhagen: H. Hagerups Forlag, 1931

Cathinca Olsen, "*Om natten hos Gandhi*" in *Indiens Venner*, 1931, no. 12, page 3.

Please see Appendix for a report on the meeting of Mrs. Hørup and Ms. Lasson with Gandhi in 1931.

Correspondence with Gandhi

Mrs. Hørup to Gandhi, May 2, 1929[535]

Rome,
May 2, 1929.

Dear *Bapujee*,

My friend, who is now in Kopenhagen, told me about a discourse, which Mrs. Menon[536] had made about you and your *ashram*. I had the impression from what she said that it is possible to be a member without living there. If it is so, I should like to know the conditions.

Here in Italy it is worse than ever after the alliance between the two blackdressed parties, the black alliance between the Pope and the dictator. None of them cares a bit for the people. To none of them it is anything else but power and politics. The one system is just like the other. Mussolini copied it exactly after the Catholic Church recognising this as the best political system in the world and adopting the holy words: He who is not with me is against me. Both of them take revenge of those who are against them prosecuting them without pity. Both of them have an army and both of them take their soldiers when they are children. Mussolini begins to train them for war, when they are but five years old. The Catholic Church lock them up in the seminaries, when they are nine. Later on, when they see what the church and their parents have prepared for them, it is almost impossible to escape. First they have lost the best years of their youth learning nothing of value neither morally nor practically. They have learned to despise everybody who thinks differently from the Catholic Church, and practically they don't know anything else but folding their hands and practise hypocrisy. Secondly, everybody would be against it: the seminary, that spend years on their education, the mother

535. SN15215.
536. Mrs. Esther (Faering) Menon.

who thought herself safe to her old age with a son who was prevented from taking a wife, and the surroundings, who saw the boy from the ninth year as a future priest in the long black uniform, and who does not like to change his opinions.

The church is now looking for the 3000 priests who have left the church and the uniform and with the help of the fascist state she will easily find them and have them lose their bread wherever they got it.

Poor Italy! It is like a ... between two nails! Ignorance and slavery are the two parties' dearest weapons.

In Denmark we have got a socialist-radical ministry. Two of my friends have been ministers-one of foreign affairs another of justice-so I hope there shall be no difficulties with my passport for India in a year and a half.

My first article about India has been published. I send you the number of the paper although it is in Danish, because I remember your expression when you asked me, "what I was doing in Rome". My second article is called "Mahatma Gandhi and his *ashram*". It is already mailed and will be published this month.

The Danish Ministry is a disarmament ministry according with my father's ideas.

I hope I have not taken too much of your time and I hope too that you will accept the photo of "San Francisco talking to the birds", which I did send you yesterday.

Your friend
Ellen Hørup

We hope for a socialist ministry in England too on the 20th of this month.

[There is a note of July 16, 1929, at the bottom of the letter that a reply (by Gandhi) was not posted for want of address.]

Mrs. Hørup to Gandhi, June 6, 1931[537]

June 6, 1931

Dear *Bapuji*,

What a joy to receive such a kind little letter from you. Thank you so very much. I had one of my bad days with headache and depression. I felt rather sick when I got it but grew quite well when I read it.

Yes, it would have been nice, if we could have met each other oftener. But I don't complain. I went to most of your meetings, and I attended more than twenty times to the evening prayer. But I always felt, that I had no right to take your time.

But now when you have been so kind to say, that you would have liked to have seen more of me in India, I will ask you to remember, that I am a Dane, and that one of our best old Danish proverbs goes: if you give the devil the little finger, he will take the whole hand.

That is what I am doing now.

I need so terrible to have a "chat" with you, as you once offered the American teachers in Allahabad. But the present situation is much more at your advantage. With the thousand miles between us you need neither to listen nor to answer. And after all I shall ask no questions. I only want to tell you the most important things people say about your going to London.

They pretend to know how well you have armed yourself for this "round table fight". First you have chosen the six best Indian experts in military, economical and commercial affairs, in Indian debts to England, in safeguards and in foreign affairs. I have only read that you have chosen five of the working committee as your companions. But people know even better than papers.

Another thing they say is that you have sent your best men to the German General Ludendorff to ask him to point out the first expert in drilling of officers and have him make a calculation

537. Rigsarkivet, Copenhagen. Courtesy, Holger Terp.

about the time necessary for Indianising the Indian army. With that paper in your pocket you will go to London, and when the Englishmen begin to speak about 20-15 years of safeguards, then you will produce that document and tell them to put that in their pipes and smoke it.

Further they say that you have decided to bring nobody but Indians with you, as you very well know, that no human is more than human, and no Englishman wants England to lose India-not even those, who see India's rights as clear as you.

Now certainly you have been filled up with people's sayings and you shall hear no more. I am on my way back to Denmark, where I shall let my friends make me a member of the board of my paper *Politiken*. During this year I shall stay in Copenhagen and try to make the paper a little less yellow and a little more truthful. If I can do nothing, I must make "The Friends of India" larger and broader and leave the others alone.

Of course I shall go to London for the "round table".

In a few months the first of my sons[538] shall be in Denmark. I gave him a Danish teacher in Calcutta, and he writes me, that he is quick to learn and will be able to go, when he receives my answer.

Yours sincerely
Ellen Hørup

Mrs. Hørup to Gandhi, November 4, 1931[539]

.....

c/o *Politiken*
Copenhagen
November 4, 1931

Dear *Bapuji*,

... letter written by Mrs. Menon to Mr. Rosenkjaer, which he wrongly told me... was written by Mirabai, there was one thing

538. Mrs. Horup adopted three boys at Miss Anne Marie Petersen's school at Porto Novo.
539. SN18243.

that impressed me very much. ... Mrs. Menon asked Mr. Roenkjaer, who had invited you to Denmark. ... answer this question by inviting you myself in the name of the Friends of India in Denmark. You can trust us. We will all of us do everything to accommodate you and your little company as well as possible.

All the societies, whose work is on line with your ideas, will join us and make every effort to arrange meetings private and public so as to give you the best opportunity to come in touch with the people you may wish to meet.

Needless to say that every expense will be met by us. We will, if it suits you, arrange a big mass meeting with an entrance fee, where the whole income will be given to you for your spinning wheels, for your hospitals or whatever purpose you may choose.

We who have been in your *ashram* know what you want and we will only be too glad to be given an occasion to show you our admiration and our love for you and for your motherland India.

I hope you will be kind enough to tell me as soon as possible if you accept this invitation and–as soon as you know it–the approximate date of your arrival.

Yours sincerely
(sd) Ellen Hørup

Mrs. Hørup to Gandhi, February 6, 1933[540]

[The Danish translation of this letter appeared in the magazine *Indiens Venner*. The original is not available. The following is a re-translation of the letter into English.] International Committee for India

Geneva
February 6, 1933

540. *Indiens Venner*, Copenhagen, 1933, No. 6, page 3.

Dear *Bapuji*,

When I tell you I am one of the two Danes who visited you at quarter past four in the morning in Kingsley Hall,[541] where we then slept in your room, then I am certain that you remember me.

I have not written to you after I left Karachi without getting the opportunity to say good-bye to you. In my last letter, I told you about the four Hindu sons I acquired during my four months residence in India, and you answered that you hoped that I got many more.

After what I have seen of you, both in India and in London, I know that you are always busy. Therefore, I thought that the best I could do was to not disturb you. But this morning something happened which gave me the desire to write to you .

Of course you can't know that I am currently living in Geneva, working as a Secretary for this committee. Neither can you know that we have decided to hold the Second International Conference for India on March 23. I have just mailed the invitations, and the acceptance letters are rolling in. When I opened one envelope, I suddenly had a letter from you in my hand. Surely, it was just a copy and it was not for me personally. But the words were yours, and they came from you. While I read your good, loving words to the violinist from Villaneuve, you came even closer to me than before.[542] And I could not resist writing to you.

541. Gandhi stayed in Kingsley Hall, a settlement house, when he visited London in 1931 to attend the Round Table Conference on constitutional reform for India, as the sole representative of the Indian National Congress.

542. The reference is to a violinist who played Bach and Beethoven for Gandhi when he visited Romain Rolland in Villeneuve in December 1931. He wrote in 1933 to Gandhi in prison, and Gandhi replied on March 7, 1933:
"I remember you well. The tones from your playing are sounding in my ears while I am dictating the letter to you....
"You don't have to be excused for your English. I am a foreigner to that language just like you. But even if I were a British erudite, I wouldn't think about the language of the correspondent, but only on the sentiment that was expressed in the language".

I wish that you know what you mean to me, and I must use a parable.

I don't know if you ever have been up in the mountains, walking an entire day without meeting a living creature. Up there, the skies and the hills meet in the horizon, and the silence together with the great emptiness brings one closer to eternity. It was in Norway I walked in the mountains, and ever since then, I think of you as my "*varde*". A *varde* is a heap of stones set up as a landmark. The stones are roughly laid upon each other to point you to the right way up in the lonely mountains where there are no roads or path you can follow--not even traces of human feet.

Travellers have built all the "vardes". They have put stone upon stone to make them high so that they can be seen from afar. It is on the right path that the world's greatest travel. And to help their fellow human beings, from getting lost, or falling into hidden abysses, they have heaped stone upon stone to show them the way.

To me, you are such a "*varde*", built by the great of humanity. You are high enough to be seen by the whole world, and I always have my eyes on you. You are the "*varde*" leading me to the right path.

Thus, I don't need to bother you often with letters. But today, when your voice sounded in my ears like the violinist in yours, I had to write.

I try the best I can to follow the path which my "*varde*" gives me, and I thank Fate for making it so high that even I...

Ellen Hørup

Gandhi to Mrs. Hørup, February 23, 1933[543]

Yeravda Central Prison,
February 23, 1933

My dear Ellen,

I was delighted to hear from you. I appreciate all your affection. I have gone up hills but I have never walked along them all day long but I do know however what you mean by the mountains reaching the horizon.

The knowledge that I am a guiding *varde* to some friends humbles me and makes me more and more conscious of the tremendous burden that I carry on my shoulders. I have to watch myself and incessantly pray to the God of Truth that I may not prove a false guide to anybody.

Yours sincerely,
Miss Ellen Hørup
Geneva

543. SN20335; *Collected Works*, Volume 53, page 378.

Mrs. Hørup to Gandhi (telegram), May 8, 1933[544]

GANDHI POONA

INTERNATIONAL COMMITTEE[545]

SENDS SYMPATHETIC GREETINGS.

HØRUP[546]

Gandhi to Mrs. Hørup, May 6, 1947[547]

Valmiki Mandir,
Reading Road,
New Delhi
May 6, 1947

Dear Ellen,

I have your letter which I was glad to receive.

I have no time to give you views.

I shall see Barbaro when she comes.

I hope your faith will never waver under the stormiest weather. Fair weather face is no face.

Love

Bapu

544. SN21224.
545. International Committee for India, Geneva.
546. Gandhi began a 21-day "self-purification" fast on May 8, 1933.
547. Source with: Holger Terp.

Appendix

Meeting of Mrs. Ellen Hørup and Ms. Caroline (Bokken) Lasson with Gandhi, February 1931[548]

[Mrs. Ellen Hørup (1871-1953), Danish journalist, and Ms. Caroline (Bokken) Lasson (1871-1970), Norwegian singer, actress and writer, visited India in the winter of 1930-31 and met Gandhi at Anand Bhavan, Allahabad, in February 1931. Gandhi had gone to Allahabad when Motilal Nehru, former president of the Indian National Congress, was ill and stayed for a few days after his death. The following is an account of the meeting by Ms. Lasson.

Mrs. Hørup and Ms. Lasson also met other Indian leaders and visited *Seva Mandir* in Porto Novo.

Ms. Lasson published a book about the journey to India, *Østens smil og tårer* ("Smiles and Tears of the East") in 1931. Ms. Lasson and Mrs. Hørup founded *Indiens Venner* ("Friends of India") in Norway and Denmark. These two organisations supported India's struggle for freedom. In 1937, they organised international support for a Nobel Peace Prize for Gandhi, but were unsuccessful.]

We were taken up the wide colonnade which goes round the whole house on the second floor, and suddenly we stood before the man towards whom the eyes of all India-nay, of all the world-are turned right now. He was sitting in the position we knew so well from photos, from calendars, from postcards and badges, with his right shoulder slightly upwards and his head down. He greeted us

548. Caroline Lasson, *Østens smil og tårer* (pages 111-18), translated by Frede Højgaard in Frede Højgaard (ed.) *Friends of Gandhi: Inter-war Scandinavian Responses to the Mahatma* (NIAS Report No. 7), 1991.

with his warm and sincere smile and asked us to sit down by his side on the carpet. My travel companion spoke about the time she had spent in his *ashram* two years ago.[549] He remembered everything, even little things that she had forgotten, and joked and laughed with a pleasant chuckle.

"What do you think of the result of the Round Table Conference,[550] Mahatmaji?" we asked.

Gandhi shook his head: "As long as I do not hear any echo out here of what they say in London, I am unable to believe that they take the question of India's freedom seriously. The ill treatment of the people continues-there is no echo here of the words spoken at the Round Table".

We did not want to keep Gandhi for too long. Before we left, we asked for permission to come to the prayer meeting, which Gandhi usually keeps open for all who want to come.

"You are most welcome! It is at seven o'clock". Then he laughed jestingly: "I also invite you to come to Morning Prayer at 4.15-but I know that you won't come then!"...

Five minutes to seven we stood on the large, open terrace above the entrance drive to Anand Bhavan, and a few minutes later came Mahatma Gandhi followed by members of the household and five to six ladies and gentlemen of the white race. From the other side came a large number of native women and men. They all took off their shoes and sandals, and we were about to do the same when Gandhi said: "You can keep your shoes on". But we took them off, the place of a prayer meeting is holy ground.

Gandhi went forward to the balustrade where a seat had been made for him of a folded rug covered with a piece of white *khaddar*. All over the balcony rugs and mats had been spread for people to sit on. We all went forward somewhat haltingly, nobody wanted to be obtrusive. "Come closer, come up here and sit down as closely as possible, there are many people here tonight-come all

549. Mrs. Horup had visited India in January 1929 and had stayed in Gandhi's *ashram* for over a week.

550. The first Round Table Conference on constitutional reform in India, at which the Indian National Congress was not represented.

the way up here so that there will be room for everybody". We followed Gandhi's friendly request and came to sit close to him on the same side as the other whites.

It was now seven o'clock. Gandhi had asked us to be punctual-what were we waiting for? Some of his followers looked at their watches. Gandhi said a few words quietly to one of Nehru's beautiful daughters-it was Pandit Motilal's elderly wife who had not yet arrived. Gandhi quietly took a watch out from under the shawl in which he was wrapped, then sat back calmly and looked ahead.

Then came the poor, old, mournful widow, half-carried by her strong son, Jawaharlal. Gandhi made room for her on his own rug, then he said a word in his quiet voice and all light was turned off-only the stars shone palely through a veil of thin clouds above us. A male voice began to sing very quietly, more and more joined in...

For a while everybody was silent, deep in his own thoughts or contemplating the stars, until Gandhi said a quiet word and the light was turned on. He bent over towards the old, grey, careworn woman by his side and said a few good and mild words to her. In reply she only uttered a syllable now and then, but we felt that the Mahatma had been able to comfort her a little for the loss of her husband, a great son of India.

Then Gandhi raises his voice and invites all the friends who had come from America, and others who felt so inclined, to follow him inside for "a little chat". We followed him into a room with no other furniture than a large rug on the floor and a spinning wheel in one corner. All over the rug there were letters and other papers. Mahatma Gandhi is a busy man. Again we took off our shoes outside, for also a home is holy ground. We sat down on the rug, behind us sat women in *saris*, directly opposite the men and the American party had grouped themselves. For a while not a word was said.

Then a lady takes courage and asks: "Would you advise us, Mr. Gandhi? How can we who strive for it, be able to follow the high ideals which you have yourself realised in such a wonderful way? We seek, and strive for what I understand is your teaching: to do good in all conditions of life. Advise us, please, how should we be able to do this?" Gandhi waits a little before he answers, then he says slowly and quietly: "Well—aren't there sufficient occasions in life to do good?—I know of no other advice than to do good whenever possible". "Yes, the occasion arises often enough, but how can we acquire the constant strength to be good, how have *you* acquired it?" "The only way I know is to have a living faith in a God who is absolutely just, a living faith in the justice of everything which comes to you in life. I don't believe in punishment and forgiveness in the normal meaning of these words. I don't believe God punishes in the same way as men or the law. And for me there is no such thing as forgiveness in the ordinary meaning of this word, forgiveness each time one happens to commit a sin. When I first read these words in the Bible, they didn't appeal to me at all, quite the opposite, I was repelled by them. But I have thought about all this and have come to the conclusion that if you understand the words in their true meaning, then they *are* true. Everybody has deserved what comes to him. But God's prisons-if he has that sort of institution-are without question educational, reforming, and they are not like human prisons. I have never met anybody who has been reformed by punishment. But if you have this living faith in the absolute justice of God, then you may be able to love even those who ill-treat you. This is now my firm opinion. And then you must practise, of course, practice makes perfect".

One of the Americans said they had been entrusted with creating a new system of education and asked Gandhi what he thought about the system in use now. Gandhi: "In my opinion the present educational system is absolutely bad! At any rate it is no good for us here in India. All these exams which you have to take are of no use whatever except for a few people who want to make their way in the world. The students are filled with a whole lot of knowledge which they had better forget again. I personally have had to unlearn a good deal of my English education, and our great friend Vallabhbhai Patel has also declared that he has thrown overboard a lot, first and foremost his English. Vallabhbhai only very rarely expresses himself in English nowadays". Gandhi looked at his English-speaking guests and laughed this hearty, internal chuckle of his.

"But all you Americans-and also Englishmen and other nations-are mostly born and brought up in towns and cities. Here in India the overwhelming part of the population live in the country. They need a completely different kind of education from those who live in the cities".

The American now asks how Gandhi thinks that education should be organised in India.

"I think we should educate young men who could go out into the villages and teach the peasants. They should teach them to cultivate their land, to grow rice and cotton, teach them to do what is right and good, and to shun what is evil. And also teach them to spin. Our villagers could be quite happy leading their simple lives. I see no reason that the 700,000 villages of India should be turned into as many cities. It won't happen in the foreseeable future, and it isn't necessary that it should happen at all. Our peasants were happy before land tax and all sorts of indirect taxes oppressed them. British history teaches us that they were happy, but British civil servants say something quite different. They can survive in their simple circumstances if they are allowed to cultivate their land in peace and earn a little extra by extra work, that is, by spinning. I don't make a fetish of the spinning wheel-if someone can come up with something better, I'll burn my *charkha* the same dav".

A bold and outspoken lady, a genuine representative of "young America", asks him the frank question what he thinks of the people of the West. Gandhi, his head down, is silent for a while. Then he bursts into a loud, infectious laughter:

"This really is a very difficult question. I have met many fine people from Western nations; they have many qualities which we don't have and which we should learn: their accuracy, their punctuality-we, for instance, don't have the same sense of time. I became friendly with a fellow prisoner once. He was English. I had to admire his deftness and inventiveness, and he made a good many practical improvements of my spinning wheel. Whether he had committed the crime he was sentenced for, I don't know-he himself thought he had been harshly treated-but even if he had done it, I wouldn't have thought twice of admitting him into my *ashram*. And a German I know-he was an engineer-him I also had to admire for his thoroughness and diligence. Undoubtedly there is much for us to learn from the people of the West, but the unhappy thing is that those who come out to India usually come as agents for either religion or automobiles".

He laughed, and everybody laughed heartily with him-it was, unfortunately, all too true, of course.

"The missionaries do much good in many ways, of course, but consciously or unconsciously, behind all this they always think of proselytising, of converting people. And now Mr. Ford, who is an excellent man, he would of course consider it his highest ambition to plant at least one motor car in each of India's 700,000 villages. That would ruin them completely".

The conversation is cheerful and lively, every word Mahatma Gandhi says comes with the power of deep conviction, but without a trace of vehemence; his way of speaking is quiet, genuine, serene.

An American suggests that we leave in order not to take more of Gandhi's time, and he answers with his lovable smile: "I was just about to make the same suggestion".

Index